LAW AND ATTITUDE CHANGE

SENATOR THURMOND: I am sure that you will agree it does not take much of a prophet to foresee an act of Congress such as this now before this committee will fail to change individual attitudes, although it is conceivable that the full force of the National Government may compel substantial compliance with the letter of the law.

MR. RUSK: I am not pessimistic, Senator, about changes in individual attitudes on questions of this sort; because so many of these individual attitudes turn on personal experience, personal discoveries about what relations can be, about situations where it becomes obvious that there can be good relations between peoples of different races and religions. And I would think one of the things that can change personal opinions would be an affirmation by the Federal Government of the great primordial doctrines of our constitutional system.

(Excerpt from the testimony of Secretary of State Dean Rusk before U.S. Senate Committee on Commerce, 88th Congress, 1st Session, hearings on S. 1732, a bill to Eliminate Discrimination in Public Accommodations Affecting Interstate Commerce, Part I, pp. 316-17, July 10, 1963.)

The strongest man is never strong enough to be always master, unless he transforms his power into right and obedience into duty.

Rousseau, *Social Contract,* II, 7

WILLIAM K. MUIR, JR.

LAW AND ATTITUDE CHANGE

THE UNIVERSITY OF CHICAGO PRESS
CHICAGO AND LONDON

This volume was originally published as *Prayer in the Public Schools: Law and Attitude Change*

ISBN: 0–226–54629–2 (clothbound); 0–226–54630–6 (paperbound)
Library of Congress Catalog Card Number: 67–28851

THE UNIVERSITY OF CHICAGO PRESS, CHICAGO 60637
The University of Chicago Press, Ltd., London

Published 1967
Phoenix Edition 1973
Printed in the United States of America

FOREWORD TO THE PHOENIX EDITION

Now that the controversy over prayers in public school is at rest, does this case study have any importance to the big problems of today and tomorrow? The answer is, decidedly yes. Every narrative is a case study, limited to a specific time and locale, but some case studies are intended to outlive their topicality. The tale of Hamlet, for example, continues to be important even though the question of the Danish succession is no longer a hot topic in conversational circles. The case of the young Danish prince retains its interest because of the timeless problems it helps us understand. People may differ in what they think Hamlet is a case of—moral conflict, the workings of an Oedipus complex, the destructive indecisiveness of a scholar who plays politics. Yet all persons agree that this incident of Danish history addresses some univeral, recurrent problem which they have had to face.

To what larger question does the story of schoolhouse religion speak? To the relationship between freedom and authority: Is coercion—the intentional use of threats to harm—a limit upon liberty, or a precondition of it? This book tells us a lot about the particular circumstances which must be present if legal authority is to enhance a free people's enjoyment of liberty and not diminish it.

Put less abstractly, here is a case of relatively successful lawmaking. I use the word "successful" advisedly because four things happened in Midland. The wrong which the legislator intended to correct was actually remedied. No vicious cycle of threat and counterthreat developed. The law was eventually accepted in Midland as tolerable and right. Lastly, the law demoralized as few Midland citizens as practically conceivable.

From this case of successful lawmaking, present and future legislators might take note of four lessons. First, and most important, if a law is to be effective, it must be framed so as to put the opportunity to enforce the law into the hands of those persons with the will to enforce it. When we talk of "will," we are speaking not only of motivation, but much more. The will to invoke the law must be strong enough to overcome the high price of insisting on one's rights—the money and time required for adequate investigation and advocacy. Moreover, will implies the personal and institutional capacity to cope with the antagonism, even hatred, of those who would nullify the law. Analysis of who actually will have the chance and the drive to uphold the law is a legislative question of critical importance. Above all else, the inclination and the opportunity to enforce the law must be made to coincide in the same persons.

Second, the enforcers of the law must have the assistance of lawyers. Lawyers in America are expected and paid to back up their clients and to buck the majority when their clients' welfare dictates that they do so. More than 135 years ago, Alexis de Tocqueville noted, "If I were asked where I place the American aristocracy, I should reply without hesitation that it . . . occupies the judicial bench and bar."[1] Today more than ever, many lawyers serve as the "aristocracy" of American politics, as Tocqueville meant the term. Their intellectual and moral training tends to oblige them to oppose the majority wisdom in their clients' interests. Moreover, thanks to their rhetorical experience, their capacity to file threatening lawsuits, and the fraternity they share with their fellow attorneys, they frequently have sufficient defenses for protecting themselves and their clients in the push-and-shove of democratic politics.

Third, the effectiveness of a specific law depends upon the self-interest of lawyers to bother with it. For example, we all know that tax laws make a great deal of difference to businessmen and government, and each side is therefore willing to compensate lawyers to become tax experts. To the extent that tax laws occasion compensation for the law profession, there is a guarantee that these laws will be enforced, interpreted, and justified with great effectiveness. Similarly, the antitrust laws and securities exchange regulations, through their multiple damage remedies, lure a class of specialized lawyers into the business of detecting and penalizing unlawful restraints of trade and

[1] Alexis de Tocqueville, *Democracy in America,* vol. 1, c. 16.

entrepreneurial frauds. Consequently, antitrust and securities laws have teeth of frightening proportions, because some lawyers have the incentive to bother.[2]

Fourth, the key to enduring social change is inventing institutions which provide legal representation to classes of people who have never had it before. The contingency fee, by which lawyers in the last century came to represent injured poor persons for a percentage of the monetary recovery, gave the working classes their first benefits of legal counsel. Indirectly but ultimately, this arrangement for compensating lawyers contributed to safer industrial conditions for the worker and improved quality control for the consumer. Likewise, the development of poverty lawyers, receiving salaries under the 1965 Economic Opportunity Act and related legislation to represent people too poor to pay for an attorney, has given social legislation considerably greater effectiveness than ever before. Free legal assistance provided impoverished persons with the capacity to exploit the opportunities to enforce the laws in their behalf.

Politics, as Ralf Dahrendorf put it so elegantly, involves "the antagonism between power and resistance."[3] A law victimizes at the very same time it benefits. Invariably some people will come to feel they have been made victims, and they will take steps to retaliate. Thus, a group benefited by laws must prepare its self-defense. If it has no lawyers to deal with the inevitable resistance, its efforts to enforce those laws will flag before long.

In a nutshell, when a legislator proposes a law, he should ask himself, *Which group of lawyers will assist in enforcing this law, in what ways, on behalf of which persons, for what reasons?* Inquiry along these lines may lead to the resolution of those truly sticky questions of employing political authority in a free society: What will be the mechanics by which the victims of a law will come to recognize its benefits? How can this legislation come to be accepted in the hearts of men? By what means can power be transformed into right, and obedience into duty?

W.K.M.

2 For example, during the 1960s Attorney Joseph Alioto, later mayor of San Francisco, earned legal fees in excess of two million dollars for bringing a successful treble-damages antitrust action against Westinghouse Electric Company on behalf of some Westinghouse customers.

3 Ralf Dahrendorf, *Essays on the Theory of Society* (Stanford, Calif.: Stanford University Press, 1968), p. 145, in his provocative essay, "In Praise of Thrasymachus."

PREFACE

Henry Luce once informally asked the political science department of his alma mater, "How do political scientists do things differently from reporters?" It was a perceptive question, and my own answer to it boils down to this: The reporter largely explains why something has happened; the political scientist, why a lot of other things did not happen instead. The principal habitat of the reporter is events; that of the social scientist, non-events.

A reporter is likely to ask why did people in Midland obey the prayer decision; the scholar will tend to deal with the question of why they did not defy it there. The point may seem at first overdrawn and indistinct: overdrawn, because the good reporter inevitably contemplates non-events (though not so many and not so systematically), indistinct, because an event and a non-event might seem to be merely counterparts. But a non-event is not simply the absence of an outcome. Defiance of the law (to return to our example) can take many forms: open incitement, passive resistance, demoralization, quitting. The political scientist's explanation—ideally at least—is geared to describe why each of various potential forms of defiance failed to materialize.

Indispensable to the political scientist is theory, which suggests the plausible non-events to explain away. Theory involves the conceptualization of a relatively few, selected causal factors and prediction of outcomes on the assumption that only the conceptualized factors are at work in the situation. When the actual outcome (legal compliance) departs from the theoretically predicted result (e.g., demoralization), the scholar has an initial inquiry: Why did not the theoretically predicted outcome occur? With the issue thus stated, he searches for the complicating cause (or causes) that "upset" the theoretical prediction. In this respect, of starting with a reliable prediction that never materialized and systematically isolating the factors that made the difference, the social scientist tends to do things differently from reporters.

Scholars have other relationships to theory than using it as an analytic tool—its creation and its proof, to mention two: creation in the sense of conceptualization, proof in the sense of validation of the predictions of the simplified situation, that is, with the marginal factors left out. (When I say the marginal factors have been left out by the theorist, I am thinking of empirical theory as George Homans does, as a purposeful simplification of the human situation in which the theorist selects only a few causal factors as basic.) The distinction between theory's creation and proof, on the one hand, and its use, on the other, is critical if the reader is to understand what psychological theory is doing in this political essay. Cognitive dissonance theory (the particular psychological formulation employed in this essay) is not used here further to create it (i.e., to develop finer concepts) or further to prove it (i.e., to improve its reliability in predicting outcomes in the laboratory situation where the only active factors are accounted for in the theory). Rather dissonance theory is being used analytically, and whether it is useful or not depends on how much our understanding is increased by the perspective it provides.

Let me state the point another way. This essay is neither an explanation of social events in dissonance theory terms nor a demonstration that dissonance theory fits the problem of legally induced attitude change more closely than other psychological theory. Creation and proof of dissonance theory are the psychologist's job, not the political scientist's. The political scientist can, however, legitimately apply psychological theory to political events in order to suppose what might have happened, but did not. One of the late President Kennedy's favorite aphorisms was the Hindu proverb, "I had no shoes, and I murmured until I met a man who had no feet." Perspective, that quality of mind which gauges events in the context of possibilities, is no less essential to the social scientist in creating explanation than it is to the statesman in developing evaluation.

In a postscript at the end of this study I have added a further word about methodology.

One word more: To thank all the many persons who instructed my thinking concerning this book might endanger the pledge of confidentiality I gave to them whose hearts and minds constitute the subjects of this book. Without naming my abettors, I know that they will see their influence and appreciate that imitation is the sincerest form of flattery. I must, however, take the opportunity to express a word of appreciation to my wife Pauli, whose discerning and sensitive eye concerning human nature continually delights and enlightens me, and to Bob Lane, who set an example.

W. K. M.

CONTENTS

CHRONOLOGY

1948—The *McCollum* case ends weekday church classes in Midland public schools

NOVEMBER, 1961—Furor over Christmas observances in adjacent Northland

JUNE, 1962—The United States Supreme Court decides *Engel v. Vitale,* prohibiting the New York State Regents' prayer

AUGUST, 1962—Furor over the Lord's Prayer in nearby Milltown

SEPTEMBER, 1962—Mayor Fiorito asks Goldman for memo on *Engel*

JANUARY, 1963—Goldman circulates confidential memo to Fiorito and the school board

FEBRUARY, 1963—First interviews begin; Supreme Court hears argument in *Schempp*

JUNE, 1963—Protestant church opinion supports Court's decision in *Engel*

JUNE 17, 1963—*Schempp* is decided, prohibiting public school "religious exercises"

JUNE 19, 1963—Midland public school summer vacation begins

JULY, 1963—State Commissioner Foley interprets *Schempp*

AUGUST, 1963—Midland school board formulates prayer ban and gets corporation counsel's approval

SEPTEMBER, 1963—Milltown and Northland school boards permit children and teachers to continue reciting prayers daily

Midland announces ban, and ban becomes a political issue in mayoralty campaign

Principal Farley mobilizes professional staff opposition to prayer ban

Mayor Fiorito wavers, then ends his indecision by recommending silent meditation while supporting board

NOVEMBER, 1963—Mayor Fiorito defeats his Republican opponent handily

State attorney general supports Midland school board and rebukes Commissioner Foley

National educational groups support Court's prayer decisions

President Kennedy is assassinated

JANUARY, 1964—Follow-up interviews begin

MARCH, 1964—School board publishes racial imbalance plan, causing new controversy

I

The Question: "Under What Circumstances...?"

Can law change deep-rooted attitudes?[1] Can legislation promote racial or religious tolerance or a democratic spirit? Can law affect the hearts of men: their feelings about themselves, their reactions toward others, their ideas about the world in which they live?

To probe these questions, I explored in some depth the attitudes of a group of educators toward schoolhouse religion—the daily recitation of the Lord's Prayer and Holy Scripture in the public schools of one American city. Assessments of their attitudes were made before and after the United States Supreme Court's decision in the *Schempp* case,[2] by which "religious exercises" in the nation's public schools were prohibited as unconstitutional. The assumption of this study was that if we are eventually to answer the grander questions posed above, we ought to start with the microscopic problem, Did *Schempp* have an effect on the attitudes of a group of educators toward schoolhouse religion?

Certainly the answer is yes for some of the respondents—John Bartkowicz and Joe Cagney, for example—although the effects were quite

[1] By "law" is meant the imperative language of a judicial (or, for that matter, legislative or executive) decision. "Attitudes" are typically defined as "predispositions to respond in a particular way toward a specified class of objects." In this book an individual's attitude will generally refer to his tendency to observe (cognition) and to evaluate (affect) some person, thing, or concept favorably or unfavorably. For further discussion, see Milton J. Rosenberg, *et al.*, *Attitude Organization and Change* (New Haven: Yale University Press, 1960).

[2] *School District of Abington Township v. Schempp,* 374 U. S. 208 (June 17, 1963).

different. Dr. Bartkowicz was a dominating man. Self-confident and physically powerful, he looked like a leader and was, in fact, superintendent of public schools in the modest-sized, Midwestern city of Midland. I met him first in March, 1963, several months before the *Schempp* decision, and talked with him about the youngsters in his school system. Ultimately he turned to religion and its importance in conveying a "sense of ethics" to schoolchildren. To leave religion out of a student's education, he argued, was like leaving "salad out of his menu: he'll survive, but he'll not survive very well." He concluded solemnly, "Man has to commune with his deity, [and] there is something good about doing it publicly."

A year later, and eight months after the Supreme Court declared that religion publicly exercised in the nation's public schools was unconstitutional, Dr. Bartkowicz talked with me again. As he had in the first interview, he asserted the importance of religion in helping "youngsters develop a sense of values." But this time, instead of emphasizing the good of schoolhouse collective prayer (as he had the year before), he scorned its importance. In his teaching career he could recall "very few instances of religious exercises having an effect on kids." The Supreme Court decision banning these innocuous rituals, far from taking away anything of consequence, actually highlighted the importance of character education and as a result had done a lot of good.

Joe Cagney was a principal in a Midland elementary school. Small and peppery, Cagney (during both occasions I was with him) gave precise and well-considered answers to my questions. As I had with Bartkowicz, I talked with Cagney several months before *Schempp*. At that time he saw prayers and Bible reading in school as overrated in their effectiveness on "discipline problems or something tangible." Despite an awareness that "we just don't give enough time to [schoolhouse religion] to influence these things," he was opposed to the suggestion that schools should provide a "special time for religious classes." The curriculum was already full of more pressing matters.

A year later (and eight months after *Schempp*), Cagney was visibly upset by the ban on morning prayers recently instituted in Midland's public schools. In contrast to Bartkowicz's composed compliance with both the letter and spirit of *Schempp*, Cagney not only castigated the decision but declared his intention to violate the law "whenever we have an opportunity to introduce some religion into the school, like at Christmas with the play—or with an Easter play." For him the necessity of schoolhouse religion was more urgent after the Supreme Court's prohibition of it than before.

Cagney and Bartkowicz were men who lived up to different responsibilities, had different friends, and held different outlooks. It was not surprising, therefore, that the clash between the law of the *Schempp* case and their original attitudes had different results. Bartkowicz's positive acceptance of the law and Cagney's negative resistance to it, however, put us on warning that the social issue to be studied is not whether law changes attitudes but rather under what circumstances law changes them positively (and under what circumstances does it not)?

If we put the question this way and then examine the body of legal and political literature, we can find descriptions and explanation of at least four distinct patterns of attitude reaction to law. The generalizations concerning these four patterns I shall call the nulist, backlash, conversion, and liberating hypotheses. (The rest of this chapter is devoted to their description.) What are the circumstances under which each of these four responses is likely to occur?

The Nulist Hypothesis

The late Justice Felix Frankfurter stated the nulist hypothesis in the following terms: "Law is concerned with external behavior and not with the inner life of man. It rests in large measure upon compulsion."[3] A person's attitudes (the "inner life of man") need not be affected by his overt conformity to the law (external behavior), even though a discrepancy exists between them. Frankfurter illustrated his point by the story of Socrates, who "lives in history partly because he gave his life for the conviction that duty of obedience to secular law does not presuppose consent to its enactment or belief in its virtue."[4] Socrates conformed to a censorship law (presumably he censored himself by drinking the hemlock) to which his belief in the virtue of free discussion was opposed, yet he changed neither his personal conviction nor his respect for the state.

Although it seems more than human for Socrates to have had no inner reaction to a legal decision compelling silence contrary to his convictions, empirical support can be found for the nulist hypothesis.

[3] *West Virginia Board of Education v. Barnette,* 319 U. S. 624, 655 (1943).

[4] *Ibid.*

Psychological theorists explain that men can comply to law and yet remain unconvinced of its virtue.[5]

Their study of cognitive dissonance deals with psychological tensions which follow the making of personal decisions (the tortures a car buyer undergoes when he has committed himself to purchasing one make of car in the face of attractive and competing alternatives). Cognitive dissonance deals with the individual's reactions to the costs of exercising choice, after his mind is made up.

These post mortem blues over foregone alternatives, so the theory goes, motivate further action. The decision maker acts to reduce his anxieties, or dissonance, over what was not done. The theorists have isolated eight distinct avenues by which this dissonance can be released. In the first place, the individual can change his mind, admit he was wrong, "uncommit" himself. Revocation may be impossible, however, if a decision has been transformed into action that cannot be undone. If a decision is irrevocable, for whatever reasons, then a person must come to terms with his decision by finding alternative avenues of eliminating his dissonance.

A second route, not unrelated to uncommitment, is for the individual to leave the field of choice and dissociate himself from the problem altogether. This course is that followed by the car buyer who sells his automobile to a second-hand dealer and rides the bus. A person who escapes from freedom of choice evades the threat of cognitive dissonance.

Third, a person may rid himself of post-decision dissonance by simply denying that attractive alternatives exist. The proverbial reluctance of some persons to shop around may be an instance of this approach to coping with dissonance. A fourth method is to depreciate the alternatives, by making them appear either less attractive or more similar to one's choice. In the case of the car buyer, he might impute

[5] Particularly those who are involved in cognitive dissonance research. Leon Festinger, *A Theory of Cognitive Dissonance* (Stanford: Stanford University Press, 1957), was the first book-length treatment of dissonance phenomena. References to the abundant work stimulated by this book can be found in Jack W. Brehm and Arthur R. Cohen, *Explorations in Cognitive Dissonance* (New York: John Wiley & Sons, 1962), pp. 319-25. I have placed heavy, nearly exclusive, reliance on the Brehm and Cohen book for the latest formulation of dissonance theory. For an example of the application of dissonance theory to political analysis, see Robert E. Lane and David O. Sears, *Public Opinion* (Englewood Cliffs, N. J.: Prentice-Hall, 1964), Chap. 5, "Leaders' Influence on Public Opinion," pp. 43-56.

to all other models a variety of defects or, alternatively, he may imagine that all the cars this year so resemble each other in every important detail that no real choice is involved. These last three avenues—dissociation, denial, and depreciation—while different in detail, all involve the common mechanism of reducing the range of choice and the options foregone. The less the choice, the less the anxiety following the choice.

The next avenue is similar to denial, dissociation, and depreciation in that the individual persuades himself that he has no choice because external compulsions prevent choice. In philosophical terms he accepts no moral responsibility for his overt action; he denies he acts of his own volition. His pattern of reaction is nulist.

The actual degree of compulsion at work is often uncertain. The formidability of the compulsion can be distorted by the person subject to it. But if the coercion seems irresistible, sufficient to satisfy him that his act is devoid of volition (and this is Frankfurter's point about law), then no or little dissonance attaches to his outward conformity to the law even though it opposes his "inner life." Compulsion acts as an escape valve for dissonance, and the reduction of dissonance reduces the individual's motivation to change his attitudes. There is thus empirical verification[6] of Frankfurter's observation. Where there is no sense of choice, a man acting in external conformity with the law may not be driven to change attitudes that are at odds with the law. A precondition of positive attitude change is a sense of volition.

The Backlash Hypothesis

More than half a century ago, in *Plessy v. Ferguson,* the Supreme Court upheld the constitutionality of state segregation statutes. In the majority opinion, Justice Henry Brown observed: "Legislation is powerless to eradicate racial instincts or to abolish distinctions based upon physical differences and the attempt to do so can only result in accentuating the difficulties of the present situation."[7] Ameliorative

[6] Experimental work has shown that a subject working under compulsion suffers much less dissonance than if he behaves, say, as a volunteer. Cohen and Brehm, summing up the findings in this field, conclude that "dissonance increases as the magnitude of the coercive force to comply decreases (where compliance is obtained)." Jack W. Brehm and Arthur R. Cohen, *Explorations in Cognitive Dissonance* (New York: John Wiley & Sons, 1962), p. 88 (Hereafter referred to as *Brehm and Cohen*).

[7] 163 U. S. 537 at 551 (1896).

legislation that runs counter to deep-rooted attitudes ("instincts") can only result in accentuating the instinctive behavior.

William Graham Sumner made the same point, holding that law invariably changed attitudes in a direction opposite the one intended. Observing that individual attitudes were determined by economic circumstances, by the "state of things,"[8] he asserted that, when lawmakers tried to compel uneconomic behavior, the individual retaliated against the legal interference, as an organism would over-react to an infection. The result was that humanitarian legislation brought about a backlash and hardened mere inclinations into determination to fight not only the law but the lawmaker.[9]

By a different explanatory route, cognitive dissonance theory predicts a similar increased animosity toward legal institutions. When an individual commits himself to behave defiantly, he undergoes considerable anxiety, for by his choice he has foregone the alternative of obedience and immunity from legal sanctions. To counter the dissonance that arises after this personal decision, he bolsters his informational and social support for defiance and invests it with deeper emotional feelings. This sixth avenue of anxiety reduction, "commitment to increased behavior of the same kind that arouses the initial dissonance,"[10] requires the individual to build up a case for fighting the policeman. The greater the penalties, the greater the risk taken by the defier; and the greater the risk, the more the dissonance, and the greater the accentuating of the defiant attitude.

In the nulist hypothesis, Justice Frankfurter noted that the more compulsion, the less effect the law had on attitudes—in cases where there is commitment to comply. Under the backlash hypothesis, the prediction is that as coercion increases, the stiffer one's opposition becomes—in cases where there is commitment to defy.[11]

[8] Sumner, *Folkways* (New York: Dover, 1959), p. 77. See chapters i-iv for general discussion of this point.

[9] Cf., Justice Murphy in his concurring opinion, *West Virginia Board of Education v. Barnette,* 319 U. S. 624, 646 (1943).

[10] *Brehm and Cohen,* p. 113.

[11] *Brehm and Cohen,* pp. 35, 56-57, describes research related to backlash effects. For example, the application of increased punishment for refusing to believe in extrasensory perception only increased the punished subject's disbelief. In another experiment, persons who sought to persuade their friends of the correctness of their point of view became more entrenched in their own attitudes the greater the degree of opposition they encountered from their friends. Leon Festinger, *A Theory of Cognitive*

The Conversion Hypothesis

Aristotle asserted that legally coerced behavior has a very definite effect on attitudes: "By doing just acts, we become just." A child who is required to behave in an outwardly "just" manner tends to be converted to a liking for justice. According to Aristotle, children develop attitudes consonant with the early habits which the state prescribes for them. Aristotle further observed that these law-induced attitudes were so profound and enduring that they could not be undone in adulthood: "It is either actually impossible, or a task of no mean difficulty, to alter by words what has been of old taken into men's very dispositions."[12] Chief Justice Warren, in the school desegregation decision, echoed Aristotle when he asserted that laws can "affect [schoolchildren's] hearts and minds in a way unlikely ever to be undone."[13]

Gunnar Myrdal, in his study of white American prejudice against Negroes, did not believe that mature attitudes were as resistant to change as Aristotle implied. He found that adult attitudes were very greatly affected by adult learning. He noted that adult whites developed unfavorable emotional responses to Negroes on the basis of their adult experience with Negro poverty.[14] If through legislation the state ameliorated the reality of Negro life, he asserted, whites would convert their hostile feelings to coincide with their more favorable observations. The difficulty in Myrdal's formulation was that he did not supply the link of motivation: why would whites pay attention to the favorable facts of Negro life? He did not meet Aristotle's point that early predispositions were likely to blind persons to changes in reality.

Cognitive dissonance supplies the motive. If an individual is induced

Dissonance (Stanford: Stanford University Press, 1957), p. 122, speculates on the importance of initial commitment to compliance: "The United States Supreme Court ruling on desegregation of schools is a case in point. The theory would imply that in those areas where compliance is obtained, that is, desegregation of schools is carried out, there would occur general opinion change toward favoring desegregation among the people. On the other hand, the theory similarly implies that in any area which does not comply, that is, successfully resists desegregation of its schools, attitudes would change in the opposite direction."

12 Aristotle, *Ethics* (trans. D. P. Chase) (New York: E. M. Dutton, 1950), p. 273.

13 *Brown v. Board of Education,* 347 U. S. 483, 494 (1954).

14 Myrdal, *An American Dilemma* (New York: Harper & Bros., 1944), p. 1066.

(but not compelled) to act in a certain way, he will search for information to support his commitment. For example, white persons induced to live in public housing through an attractive rental schedule will be attentive to anything which mitigates misgivings about the decision, one source of which might be the racial integration measures to which public housing is subject. Dissonance theory would predict that whites who had a prior reluctance to associate with Negroes would be highly motivated to convert their attitudes. Conversion would consist of developing a liking for Negroes and of searching for supportive information that the law has had a good effect. This conversion of attitude would eliminate previous anxiety about the decision to place their families in integrated public housing.[15]

The crucial point is that legal compulsion incurred as an incident to a prior free choice creates cognitive dissonance, which in turn motivates positive attitude change. This seventh avenue of dissonance reduction—conversion to feelings, beliefs, and associations which justify the initial commitment—suggests that law may very effectively alter attitudes. Furthermore, the subtle implications of the conversion hypothesis is that the more unfavorably persons are disposed to the law at the outset, the more troubled they are by their commitment and the more attitude change will occur eventually.[16]

The Liberating Hypothesis

Law, according to the fourth generalization, liberates the individual from the anxieties of indecision and equivocation. If we, like Chester Barnard,[17] take as axiomatic that men hold several possibly contradictory attitudes on any one subject, we can imagine circumstances suddenly causing an acute moral competition within an individual. The law can affect the outcome of that competition.

[15] On conversion, see M. Deutsch and M. Collins, *Interracial Housing* (Minneapolis: University of Minnesota Press, 1951); D. M. Wilner, R. P. Walkley and S. W. Cook, *Human Relations in Interracial Housing* (Minneapolis: University of Minnesota Press, 1955).

[16] *Brehm and Cohen,* p. 273: "The more unfavorable are persons toward a position or an event, the more dissonance and consequent attitude change they experience on commitment to that event. Thus, we should expect that whites, who through some exercise of choice, have become committed to interaction with Negroes, would change their attitudes toward Negroes more in the favorable direction, the more unfavorable they were to begin with."

[17] Chester I. Barnard, *The Functions of the Executive* (Cambridge, Mass.: Harvard University Press, 1938), Chap. 17.

Let us imagine a man who is a white American, a devoted citizen of Georgia, and a Roman Catholic, who has a wife and several children. He manages a large hotel in Atlanta in competition with other hostelries within the city. Let us suppose, further, that his religion has left him with a positive feeling toward the idea of universal equality and that his education has informed him that desegregation is likely to alleviate bigotry and poverty. In accordance with his religious feeling and his intellectual expectations, he would integrate his hotel. Yet he believes that were he to do so, his clientele would patronize competing (segregated) hotels, his hotel colleagues would no longer respect him, his home would be dynamited, and his friends would spurn his wife and children.

So long as there is no law to guide his choice between his moral and local attitudes, civil rights agitation imposes on our hotelkeeper an acutely important psychological dilemma. Any choice involves severe costs.

Let us further suppose that an effectively enforced civil rights law is legislated. His predicament is resolved. By coercing all the hotels in the area to desegregate, the law eliminates segregation as a factor in the competition between them. If public officials praise his acts to integrate as those of a responsible, law-abiding citizen and jail extremists who might retaliate against him—if, in short, the law eliminates the vicious consequences of his favoring integration—he is relieved of the anxieties caused by the conflict in his attitudes. At the same time, however, he might well become less concerned about the moral principle of racial tolerance, subordinating it to a position of less importance than, say, reasserting his community solidarity.

The parallel of the liberating hypothesis in cognitive dissonance theory is found in the fact that a man with equivocal attitudes suffers extreme dissonance, for any choice requires him to oppose at least a part of his belief system. The absence of law drives him to resolve the attitudinal equivocation and terminate his discomfort. But if the law perceptibly reduces the negative attributes of one horn of the dilemma, dissonance is reduced, leaving him less motive to modify the original equivocation. Law makes the choice less urgent and relegates his commitment to integration to a "zone of indifference."[18] Under circumstances where there is commitment to comply, the less important the decision comes to appear, the less positive the attitude change. Dimin-

[18] *Ibid.*, p. 167.

ishing the importance of the consequences of a decision in turn diminishes the drive to change the original equivocal attitude.

To summarize: We have identified four patterns of legally-induced attitude change explicit in the legal and political literature.

The nulist hypothesis.—Under circumstances where the individual commits himself to compliant behavior, the more the compulsion, the less positive the attitude change.

The backlash hypothesis.—Under circumstances where the individual commits himself to defiant behavior, the more the compulsion, the more negative is the attitude change.

The conversion hypothesis.—Under circumstances where the individual commits himself to compliant behavior, the more volition perceived, the more positive the attitude change if the importance of the decision remains constant.

The liberating hypothesis.—Under circumstances where the individual commits himself to compliant behavior, and if the perception of volition remains constant, the less important the decision appears, the less positive the attitude change.

If to these four patterns we add the four other, distinctly less important, possibilities suggested by dissonance theory, we have eight possible reactions to the law when the verbal imperative is inconsistent with an individual's original attitudes. He may deny the existence of the law, depreciate it by interpreting it to be inapplicable, dissociate himself from the field covered by the law, become indecisive, keep the original attitude and exaggerate the coercive effects of the law (nulist); he may accentuate the original attitude and derogate the law (backlash); he may convert to the legal attitude (conversion); or he may diminish the importance of eliminating an originally equivocal attitude (liberating). The job ultimately is to define more accurately the circumstances under which an individual will choose one or the other of these eight reactions.

II

The Setting: *Schempp* and Midland

In the half year preceding the Supreme Court's decision in *Schempp*[1] twenty-nine members of the Midland public school system were interviewed. The respondents comprised the entire seven-member school board, the superintendent and the associate superintendent, and a one-in-two random sample of the system's forty-one principals. (One white Catholic male principal was excused because of a death in the family. No replacement was made.) Each interview consisted of the identical fifty-two questions and ran from forty minutes to four hours, the median being ninety minutes, not including interruptions. The questions dealt with the respondents' liking for their jobs, their direct experience with legal institutions, their knowledge of the Supreme Court, their political predispositions, and their attitudes about religious observances in the public schools. Interviews were also conducted with the headmasters of the five non-sectarian private schools in the Midland area, using an abbreviated questionnaire consisting of thirty-eight questions pertaining to knowledge of the Supreme Court, political attitudes, and preferences in the matter of schoolhouse religion.

Eight months after *Schempp*, reinterviews were begun with twenty-eight of the twenty-nine original public school respondents. (One white Protestant woman principal retired at the end of the preceding aca-

[1] Hereafter I shall speak of the June 17, 1963, decision variously as "*Schempp*," the "prayer cases" and the "prayer decision." (The phrase, "prayer ban," will refer to the local implementation of *Schempp*, the regulation issued by the Midland School Board to carry out *Schempp* in the Midland schools.)

demic year and was dropped from the sample.) The second interviews lasted approximately the same length of time as the original ones, and consisted of forty-four questions dealing with the educators' formal and informal social relationships within the system, their reactions to the prayer cases, and their current attitudes about religious observances in the classrooms. The five private school headmasters also were reinterviewed, with an abbreviated questionnaire limited to their personal reaction to *Schempp* and their current attitudes about religious training in their schools.

Since the private headmasters were not employees of government, they and their schools were not legally affected by the Supreme Court's ban on prayers, which applied only to public schools. They were included in the study as a crude kind of control group, significantly similar to the experimental group (the twenty-eight public school respondents) except in respect of their exemption from the law.

For the most part these conversations were conducted in the private offices of the persons interviewed during working hours, although some took place in homes in the evening or on weekends and a few were conducted at meals. In each case, handwritten notes, as complete as possible, were taken of every answer during the interview itself, and verbatim reconstructions were made of the complete conversation upon departure. Assurances of anonymity were given before every interview; each respondent was told that the name of the city would be disguised, he would be given a pseudonym, and other identifying information would be altered insofar as it was non-essential to the inquiry. I prefaced each of the original interviews by telling the respondent I was interested in his opinion of the American Supreme Court. The follow-up interview was justified in terms of the Court's recent decision in *Schempp,* which directly affected them and might have affected their feelings about the Court; hence, I was obliged to return to bring my study up to date.

Before we see what the interviews revealed about the process of legally induced attitude change, let us quickly detail their legal and local setting. What was the *Schempp* decision? And what was Midland like?

Abington Township v. Schempp

Schempp was a decision resolving two separate law suits joined by the Supreme Court for purposes of judicial efficiency. One suit, *Abington*

Township v. Schempp,[2] was begun by two Unitarian teenagers who attended a suburban secondary school near Philadelphia. The plaintiff in the second case, *Murray v. Baltimore,*[3] was a professed atheist who attended a large Baltimore public high school. The two Schempps and Murray, after complaining to the various school officials about the devotional ceremonies with which their schools began each day, had taken their objections to local law courts and, eventually, to the United States Supreme Court. What they disliked were the daily recital of the Lord's Prayer and reading of the Bible. The Supreme Court heard their complaints and the arguments of their adversaries late in February, 1963, and on the following June 17 announced its decision to sustain the students.[4]

The three youngsters were able to involve the courts because they alleged that the exercises violated the Fourteenth Amendment of the Constitution of the United States, which provides in part that "No State shall . . . deprive any person of life, liberty, or property, without due process of law." The Court's ruling became the law of the land. Its imperative language provided that "religious exercises . . . are . . . in direct violation of the rights of the [plaintiffs]."[5] Public school officials were forbidden to authorize "religious exercises" on school premises.

Others in the past had invoked the courts to protect their liberty of belief. When a young Jehovah's Witness couple objected to a West Virginia law which required their child to salute the American flag, the Supreme Court, in *West Virginia Board of Education v. Barnette*[6] (1943), abrogated the statute because it required the ritual of all school children regardless of their beliefs.

In another case, *Illinois ex rel. McCollum v. Board of Education*[7] (1948), a mother whose child attended public school complained of local public school officials who permitted sectarian church school teachers to conduct religious courses on public school premises during public school hours. The Supreme Court sustained her and ordered

[2] (E. D. Pa., 1959) 177 F. Supp. 398; judgment vacated, 364 U. S. 298 (1960); motion granted to amend pleadings, (E. D. Pa., 1961) 195 F. Supp. 518; (E. D. Pa., 1962) 201 F. Supp. 815.

[3] 228 Md. 239, 179 A. 2d 698 (1962).

[4] *School District of Abington Township, Pa. v. Schempp,* 374 U. S. 208 (1963).

[5] 374 U. S., at 224.

[6] 319 U. S. 624 (1943).

[7] 333 U. S. 203 (1948).

that there be no "utilization of the tax-established and tax-supported public school system to aid religious groups to spread their faith."[8]

Relying on this tradition of judicial activity in matters of church and state, the two Schempps and Murray had asked the courts to review the constitutionality of daily devotionals. It is important to note that the religious exercises involved were not compulsory. Under the Pennsylvania and Baltimore practices, no official penalties coerced the students to participate (in contrast to the flag salute in *Barnette*). Formally, the plaintiffs had the opportunity to leave the classroom during the exercises. Nonetheless, the Supreme Court ruled that the option to abstain did not provide due process of law.

What constitutes due process of law in the area of religious liberty? More than two decades ago the Supreme Court said that state and local officials violated the due process clause of the Fourteenth Amendment in matters touching religious liberty whenever they acted in ways explicitly forbidden to federal officials by the First Amendment. The religious safeguards provided by the First Amendment are that "Congress shall make no law respecting an establishment of religion, or prohibiting the free exercise thereof." Thus, under the Court's interpretation of the Fourteenth Amendment, if a local government agency made a policy "respecting an establishment of religion" or "prohibiting the free exercise" of religion, the "State" deprived persons of their liberty of belief without due process.[9]

Lawyers speak of the First Amendment as being "incorporated"[10] into the Fourteenth, meaning that local and federal officials must conform to the same constitional standards in religious matters. Because both the establishment and free exercise clauses apply to local officials by virtue of this incorporation, the Schempps and Murray were able to complain about the non-compulsory devotionals as establishing a form of worship in their public schools.

As far as public school ceremonies were concerned, the practical

[8] In *Doremus v. Board of Education,* 342 U. S. 429 (1952), plaintiffs raised the same substantive issues as were raised in *Schempp*. The appeal, however, was dismissed by the Supreme Court upon the graduation of the school child involved and because of the parents' failure to establish standing to sue as taxpayers.

[9] *Cantwell v. Connecticut,* 310 U. S. 296, 303 (1940).

[10] Glendon Schubert has a useful paragraph on the meaning of the concept, "incorporation." *Constitutional Politics* (New York: Holt, Rinehart and Winston, 1960), pp. 528-29.

difference between applying the establishment instead of the free exercise clause was the avoidance of the pressures of social conformity within the classroom. If a ceremony was judged in terms of whether it curtailed the free exercise of religion, it could be introduced into the school on a voluntary basis, as the flag salute was. Then, as a practical matter, the approval of contemporaries and teachers would become a strong inducement to a schoolchild to forego his "intellectual individualism"[11] and to volunteer to participate. If the ceremony was forbidden as an establishment of religion, it could not be introduced into the classroom in any circumstances, even on a voluntary basis, and the schoolchild thus avoided the dilemma of having to assert his liberty of belief at the expense of his social acceptability. The eccentricities of his personal religious faith were never put in issue.

By the time the Schempps and Murray brought their complaints to the Supreme Court, the *Barnette* and *McCollum* decisions had already drawn a distinction between patriotic exercises (which were permitted on a voluntary basis) and practices of worship (which were forbidden in the public schoolroom). As recently as 1962, the Court had applied this distinction in *Engel v. Vitale*,[12] to prohibit as an establishment of religion the optional recital of a non-denominational prayer composed by the New York State Board of Regents and which recited, "Almighty God, we acknowledge our dependence upon Thee, and we beg Thy blessings upon us, our parents, our teachers and our country." The uniqueness of the particular prayer, however, divested the *Engel* decision of widespread impact. Technically, no Supreme Court decision governs parties other than those directly involved in the litigation. Yet, by dint of established political and legal traditions, officials and lawyers tend to treat decisions concerning facts legally indistinguishable from matters in which they are involved as binding on them as well. This act of cooperation saves time and generally preserves political and legal reputations.

As a devotional composed by political officials and not by private persons, however, the New York Regents' prayer was distinguishable from the Lord's Prayer and the Holy Bible. Lawyers generally agreed that *Engel* did not cover religious exercises which were not state-

[11] Justice Jackson, *West Virginia Board of Education v. Barnette,* 319 U. S., at 641.

[12] 370 U. S. 421 (1962).

composed.[13] In the absence of a clear precedent, the Schempps and Murray had had to pursue their cases to the Supreme Court. The decision in their cases which prohibited the recital of the Lord's Prayer and Bible reading unquestionably covered Midland in this cooperative sense; throughout the Midland public school system, the Bible was being read and the Lord's Prayer was traditionally and daily recited.

Midland

In 1963 Midland was a city of about two hundred thousand with nationality backgrounds which were Polish, Irish, Italian, Jewish, white Protestant, and Negro. Sixty per cent of its population was Catholic, another 15 per cent Jewish, and the remainder Protestant or not affiliated. It was surrounded by suburbs—Northland and Milltown, to mention two—which were less Catholic and more Protestant than Midland proper.

Midland was a city of skilled labor. Its industry was increasing, and economic hopes were high. In 1963 Midland's inhabitants had a per capita income below the national average (but not much) and an educational level below the national norm (but not much).

The city had two evenly matched political parties, although for a decade a Democrat named Anthony Fiorito had occupied the mayor's office. Despite Fiorito's success, the tradition of two-party politics and the generally moderate views of Republican candidates meant that the Democrats always had formidable opposition.

Midland also had several institutions of higher learning, including Teacher's College, which had a good reputation, and the prominent, publicly supported University of Midland. Its public school system annually educated twenty thousand students. While more than half of its graduates went on to college, substantial weaknesses remained unremedied; a recent national study showed that the bottom quarter of its grade schoolers were substantially below the national 25th percentile level.

Nine parochial schools including a high school had been built in Midland, and 20 per cent of Midland's school-age population attended them, representing a gradual increase over the past decade. Midland's

[13] For a scholarly and lawyerlike commentary on the *Engel* case, see Paul G. Kauper, "Prayer, Public Schools and the Supreme Court," *Michigan Law Review,* 61 (1963), 1043-44.

five non-sectarian private schools—expensive, selective, and stable in size—were predominantly white Protestant, though not exclusively so.

Schoolhouse Religion in Midland

Beginning in the 1920's throughout the Midland area, a trend to increase religious training in the public schools set in, continuing until 1948. In that year, in response to the Supreme Court's *McCollum* decision, weekday church classes were prohibited on school premises, and the morning ceremony for each school was in the main limited to the recital of the Lord's Prayer. Bible reading, though common in the high schools and the predominantly Protestant primary schools, was non-existent in primary schools with heavy Catholic populations.

During the next decade, in response to complaints chiefly by Jewish groups, the teachers, principals, and school board acted quickly to restrain individual acts of religious overzealousness within the classrooms. So far as can be determined, schoolhouse religion—at least the daily saying of the Lord's Prayer—was generally popular and accepted as traditional and appropriate.

In November, 1961, in adjacent Northland a Jewish group made public its grievances over the extent of the Christmas observances in the public schools and asked that they be curtailed. The complaint led to the calling of a public meeting, which aroused such bitter religious animosities that the Jewish group withdrew its request.

Within a year, however, the *Engel* case focused national attention on schoolhouse religion. In New York, as one consequence, the state commissioner of education acted decisively to eliminate the Regents' prayer and all other religious vestiges from public school classrooms.

Thereafter a few residents in Milltown, a suburb near Midland, sought the elimination of religious observances from the public schools on the basis of *Engel*. The kind of bitterness which had erupted in Northland the year before again broke out in the public meetings on the matter, and again no change in policy was effected.

The Midland school board took no public action as a result of the *Engel* case, but Mayor Fiorito requested one of the school board members, a lawyer named Frank Goldman, to prepare a confidential memorandum on the implications of the case. In January, 1963, the report was submitted to Fiorito and, separately but also confidentially, to the school board. While acknowledging that in *Engel* the Supreme Court "did not . . . have occasion" to discuss exactly the kind of devotionals in general use in Midland schools, Goldman made it clear that in his judgment the Court "will conclude that recitation of the Lord's Prayer in the classroom likewise violates the constitutionally required separation of church and state." "We would do well," he urged, "to give some advance thought as to what remedial steps we may want to take when a decision is inescapably upon us." Under Goldman's prodding the board intermittently returned to the issue of devotional ritual, sandwiching in discussion between such pressing tasks as altering the curriculum and formulating a controversial plan to redress racial imbalance.

In the winter of 1963 my first interviews took place. Although the *Engel* decision of the preceding summer had troubled many of Midland's public school teachers, when the school board took no action to ban prayers in the fall of 1962, teachers generally began to think that the threat of a prayer ban had passed forever. This wishful thinking was encouraged by educational journal articles discussing *Engel.* Typically these articles concluded quite differently from Goldman, "It is extremely unlikely that school practices relating to non-sectarian prayers will be seriously affected."[14]

On February 27 and 28, 1963, *Schempp* was argued in the Supreme Court. In the three months before the Court announced its decision, Protestant support at the national level for the *Engel* decision was mobilized: the National Council of Churches and various sectarian groups commented favorably on the Court's philosophy of separation of church and state, thus concurring with national Jewish groups. National Catholic spokesmen were quiet. On June 17, 1963, the prayer cases were announced in the newspapers, crowded in with such eye-catching items as the death of Pope John, the election of Pope Paul, and the increasing momentum of the civil rights movement.

Meanwhile, the Midland school board was getting into hot water. Its efforts to upgrade the educational standards of the school system created suspicion and hostility among some of the staff. Dr. Bartkowicz, the new superintendent of schools, brought in from the outside, made several indiscreet remarks which Republicans capitalized on to embarrass Mayor Fiorito. Summer vacation, beginning on June 19, relieved some of the pressure, but summer wrought havoc on the school board's hopes of settling the matter of school prayers dispassionately. The local congressman stressed his unhappiness with the *Schempp* decision. The state commissioner of education, Martin

[14] E.g., Sam Duker, "The Supreme Court Ruling on School Prayers," *The Educational Forum,* 27 (1962), 71-77.

Foley, delivered himself of several off-the-cuff interpretations of it. ("If teachers . . . and schoolchildren want to say [prayers], so what? They're a traditional sort of thing.") And throughout the state most school systems made no attempt to ban traditional religious practices.

The Midland school board met the issue head-on, formulating a policy to comply with the Supreme Court's rule. By August, Goldman's draft of the prayer ban had the approval of the school board and had been cleared with the city's corporation counsel (and presumably with Mayor Fiorito). It read simply:

> To maintain absolute religious liberty for all Americans and to comply with recent decisions of the Supreme Court of the United States, employees of the Midland public schools shall not conduct, or authorize students to conduct, prayers or other devotional exercises on school premises.

When the board announced its policy on September 9, two days after the resumption of classes, all kinds of opposition stirred. It was election time, and the Republicans called for the ouster of the school board. Within the school system itself, one elementary school principal, Farley, organized the Committee for Retention of School Prayers and obtained four thousand signatures on a petition. The independent labor organization, the Teachers' Association, sought the advice of legal counsel.

By the end of September the lawyer for the association, Jim Holden, advised the teachers that the board's position was unimpeachable and that State Commissioner Foley's opinion was absurd; countervailing groups supporting the prayer ban were formed; and the Republican candidates were badly divided on the propriety of attacking the school board on the issue. Mayor Fiorito, after conferring with Goldman, Associate Superintendent Miss O'Hara, and others, broke his silence by writing a letter to the school board in which he cited Justice Brennan's concurring opinion in *Schempp* and suggested consideration be given to the "observance of a moment of silent meditation at the beginning of each school day." The letter received a favorable response from the usually anti-Fiorito press, and one of the leading Knights of Columbus publicly said silent meditation was a good idea. The crisis passed, and new issues—patronage, economics, and racism—crowded the prayer ban out of the election picture. In November, Fiorito beat his Republican opponent in a landslide.

In the middle of November, the state attorney general rebuked

Foley's interpretation of the *Schempp* case and supported the Midland school board unequivocally. His opinion accorded with those of attorneys general in other states. The national PTA and the National Education Association also gave their support to *Schempp*.

The assassination of President Kennedy on November 22 brought a moratorium on the attacks against the Midland school board, but within three months the board was again engulfed in controversy when it released a racial imbalance plan to deal with de facto segregation in the elementary schools. In the middle of this controversy the follow-up interviews were completed.

These were the highlights of the story of the prayer ban in Midland. To this common historical context every Midland public school educator was exposed. It is now time to describe some of those educators and to explain the impact of the events of the controversy on their personal attitudes.

III

The Personnel

The Midland school system included more than one thousand personnel. It included members of the school board, superintendents, supervisors, principals, teachers, coaches, custodians, bus drivers, and cooks. In fact, many more persons were part of Midland's educational organization—P.T.A. leaders, the city's board of estimate, crosswalk guards, consulting psychiatrists, municipal social workers, religious leaders, the city council, the mayor, not to mention the students. While their names did not appear as an official part of the system, many of these persons were extremely influential within it.

My study focused on three particular groups of administrators in the Midland school system which occupied positions of attention within the organization and which made, or at least ratified, many of the important decisions: the school board, the superintendents, and the principals.

The interviewed members of these three groups numbered twenty-eight. They were sixteen men and twelve women, twenty-six whites and two Negroes. Their ages ranged from thirty-five to sixty-eight, with most in their forties and fifties. Not only had they gone to college; each had received postgraduate education (three were Ph.D.'s). Twenty-one were professional secondary educators (none of the seven persons on the school board was paid for his service, but two had been secondary teachers and another was a university professor). All were native-born; most had been raised in Midland.

Eighteen were Catholics, six were Jews, and four were Protestants. Of the Catholics, eleven were Irish in their national background, six were Italian, and one was Polish.

A quarter of them was registered with a political party (five Democrats, two Republicans). The domestic political attitudes of the twenty-eight tended to be liberal—that is, they were likely to have favorable attitudes toward labor, the welfare state, and government regulation of business. On a three-item modified version of Centers' Liberalism-Conservatism measure,[1] twelve were liberals, seven were conservatives, and nine were middle-of-the-roaders.

The School Board

The seven school board members had been appointed by the mayor for overlapping terms. They were young, married, parents; Mrs. Hanna, the one woman on the board and a university professor, was the only one with children of college age. They were predominantly liberals; the two conservatives were Coleman, a Negro social worker, and Dr. Timothy Clancy, an Irish pediatrician. Three—Mrs. Hanna, Coleman, and Leonard, a manufacturer—were Protestants, although Mrs. Hanna and Coleman were nominal ones. Derzon, a retailer, and Goldman, a lawyer, were Jewish. Dr. Clancy and Chairman Rizzuto, an educational aids specialist, were Catholic. Rizzuto and Derzon were both graduates of and former teachers in the Midland school system, while Mrs. Hanna and Dr. Clancy were graduates of the system. At the time of the first interview, only Rizzuto had served more than one term, having been on the board seven years.

The board members were surprisingly well informed about the Midland school system, their knowledge being based not only on their better-than-weekly meetings but also on first-hand familiarity with the schools. Professor Hanna's personal responsibility was upgrading the high school language programs, and she frequently sat in on classes. Leonard's avocation was concern for better science education, which took him into all the schools. Coleman, as a social worker, mixed with Negro students attending both senior high schools, two of the four junior high schools, and four of the elementary schools. Rizzuto's personal friends were largely school teachers, and his job as an educational aids specialist took him into school systems throughout the Midwest. And so on.

The morale of the school board—that is, their willingness as individuals to give abundantly to the group effort—was high, by any measure. Although the members received no salary, Goldman, a man of abundant obligations, said, "It's been a revelation, a whole new

[1] See Appendix for further discussion of index.

situation." The members used terms like "demanding," "a chore," and "really getting out of hand" to describe their commitment to the board, but in the next breath came adjectives like "wonderful," "creative," and "rewarding." They liked each other; every one of the seven spontaneously gave details about the personalities and attitudes of their fellows, always with humor and respect.

Furthermore, they enjoyed a respect within the school system itself. The two superintendents spoke of them as "courageous, intelligent, alert" and "men with extraordinary talents." The brashest of the principals echoed the preponderant sentiment among the staff when he said that the board members "really know what are the modern educational problems of modern educational systems."

Rizzuto and Leonard

By narrowing our focus to two board members, we may give depth to our understanding of the school board in the Midland community. We selected the board chairman, the Catholic Rizzuto, and the outspoken manufacturer, the Protestant Leonard. Each man was in his forties; each had children presently in the school system; each was a former secondary school teacher; and each was liberal in his domestic politics.

Rizzuto was a small, wiry Italian, with an athlete's build and a picaroon's smile. He had spent his entire life in Midland, the son of a newspaperman, the product of Midland parochial and public schools and a graduate of the local University of Midland. He made his home in Forest Hill, a mixed Catholic and Jewish neighborhood in Midland, a short block from the Catholic church and parochial school. He made friends readily, enjoyed sports, and admired the mayor of Midland, who happened to live nearby. He was a registered Democrat. He loved politics, politicians, and people who liked politics. If imitation is the sincerest form of flattery, then he paid his respects to the late President Kennedy by writing a school history book that consciously paralleled the biographical *Profiles in Courage*.

Rizzuto and his wife, who was also a former school teacher, had innumerable friends. The only member of the school board with extensive acquaintance among the public school staff, he was a member of the Knights of Columbus and a loyal churchgoer. His business office was in a nearby larger city. As a result he knew a regular crowd of commuters, with whom he discussed the events of the day. He thought methodically, in detail and aloud, preferring debate with others over meditation by himself. In short, he was a man who admired intellect, courage, and physical skill, socialized easily and often, was tolerant and prided himself in his tolerance. On the board he was the moderator; "he just keeps us going," Coleman, the social worker, put it.

Rizzuto was a faithful Catholic. "I say this without trying to be immodest, but I am a pretty devout and religious man; as far as my religion goes, I try hard to practice it faithfully." "Religion," said Professor Hanna simply, "is meaningful to him."

Rizzuto, with his devout life, his devout home, and his devout background, faced in the prayer issue the knowledge that his wife, his friends, his social groups, his church, even his former schoolteachers, were arrayed against banning prayers from the public schools. As a result of the prayer ban, the president of the Knights of Columbus had "quite a set-to" with him. He had to "part company for good" with a friend who called the lawyer Goldman a Communist. Teachers accused Rizzuto of being "godless." Friends "acted differently toward me for a few weeks." He and his family received "forty or fifty" telephone calls from extremists who "heaped into the telephone real filth." Like marmalade to bees, Rizzuto attracted outspoken criticism from every quarter. Yet, by dint of habit, Rizzuto sympathized with the citizenry.

So many people shared my misgivings about ruling out prayer . . . A doggone sizeable majority was scared that the world was going to hell in a handbasket, and that a little God in the schools was all that lay between us and perdition. If they take that away, what will happen to the morality of all the kids? I think it was a shortsighted view, but this prayer ban devolved upon the community so suddenly . . . They had been preoccupied during the summer with whether the Pirates would win the pennant, and whether the new coach at Midland would have a winning football team in his first season, and there was Cuba and all that, and all of a sudden the public realized that here was a decision about to be made ruling out prayers. And it was a crisis that they reacted emotionally to.

He searched about for any break in the unanimity of the adverse reaction he confronted. The support of a Republican councilman, even the reaction of a television interviewer, bolstered his spirit. And when the attorneys general of other states insisted on the elimination of devotions in their public schools, he read every word of their opinions as "an authority we could point to."

Leonard, of the same age and liberal persuasion, made a sharp contrast. He was a stocky, powerful man, with a square head and piercing eyes. His father had been a farmer in upper New York state and a Congregationalist in his religion. Leonard had left the farm, taught in Midwestern high schools, received a Ph.D., and been a science teacher at several universities. He had never studied or taught in any school where prayers had been recited. Leonard had gone to work for a national manufacturer and thirteen years ago had come to Midland. He lived in a white Protestant neighborhood. He worked egregiously long hours, purposely restricting his occasions for socializing, apparently with the ready consent of his wife. He was not a registered political party member. "I make it a practice not to visit" any members of the school system except on business.

His wife opposed schoolhouse religion in the public schools; so did his friends. To Leonard the community reaction to the prayer ban was "quiet." His personal contacts with the school staff on the issue were limited to talking with "five or six principals and teachers about it." There were no threatening phone calls, and any letters on the subject were dispatched to the trash barrel. His knowledge of the community's reaction was second-hand, through newspapers. Beyond extensive talks with Goldman, the lawyer on the board, he was acquainted with the thinking of lawyers only through his self-exposure to comment in the legal journals.

His personal acquaintance was selective and parochial, but Leonard was a man insulated from local reaction as much by his personality as by his social circles. His reputation was highly intellectual and forbidding. One superintendent, who admired him, described him as "sharp" and "grating." Leonard prided himself in his imperviousness to what others thought of him; "men," he said, can be "too much sensitive to public opinion."

But the opinions of others did matter to Leonard. He had his public. The esteem of his colleagues on the board, especially Goldman, counted. So did the imagined praise of Justice William Douglas, "one of my heroes"; of Professor Burr from his Cornell college days; and of all the people that constituted "my own bringing up." These men and women were those to whom Leonard was accessible—his public.

Rizzuto and Leonard represented the extremes on the school board in their local accessibility. While Rizzuto's public was largely within Midland, Leonard's was outside the city limits. Yet they were alike in an important respect. Each had to "live with" his relevant public. Each would have felt a twinge of estrangement at best, and disloyalty at worst, if he departed too radically from the opinions of the men and women he valued.

Of the other board members, Dr. Clancy, the neighborhood pediatrician, was very much like Rizzuto. Lawyer friends insisted on pointing out the loopholes in the Supreme Court's decision; every social party turned into an argument; every phone call came in opposition; no one ever said, "Timmy, we are proud of you, the way you took that stand." But, by and large, Rizzuto and Clancy were the only two board members with communication lines sufficiently exposed to be touched by a hostile public reaction. Derzon in his Jewish circle and Coleman in the Negro community did not tune in the reaction of the Irish and the Italian Catholics. And somehow no one dared to speak back to Goldman and Mrs. Hanna; their own personal skills of articulation, or at least their reputation as talkers, put people off.

The Superintendents

To be a school superintendent in Midland was to be lonely. He was set apart from the principals and classroom staff, physically by his offices in the city hall, and socially by his status. He was separated by background and professional subordination from the school board. He had little friendly association with interested parents, small children, grateful alumni, enthusiastic teachers, or problematic neighborhoods. He was a troubleshooter, ranging over a wide array of problems, offering solutions but needing others to implement them. If he talked, everyone listened; there was little room for indiscretion.

The two superintendents of the Midland school system, one with ultimate jurisdiction and the second with responsibility for the elementary schools, were Dr. Bartkowicz and Miss Mary O'Hara. They worked closely with the school board, Bartkowicz playing the dominant part but Miss O'Hara frequently substituting when Bartkowicz was sick or absent. Both were much respected by the board, but it was Bartkowicz who obtained its especial attention, and it was for him that Professor Hanna reserved the accolade "top-notch." Articulate, liberal, and intelligent, these two superintendents had quite different self-images—sufficiently different to produce what Miss O'Hara called a parting of the ways between them.

Bartkowicz and O'Hara

John Bartkowicz was in his very early fifties. As I said before, he was a big man, standing six feet three, with a massive forehead and huge hands. He worked hard, talked confidently, and made the world spin around his ego.

He had been born in a middle-sized town in northern Michigan of

Polish-American parents; his father was an engineer and a Catholic in a predominantly Protestant community. Although Bartkowicz went to parochial elementary schools, he took part in non-Catholic boyhood activities—for example, the Boy Scouts. He went to the local public high school and the state university.

Bartkowicz came to Midland in September, 1962, less than a year before the Supreme Court decided *Schempp.* He had received his early experience in the school systems of small Midwestern towns, from which he brought a reputation for innovation and decisiveness. In the Midland system he remained aloof. He refrained from joining staff social organizations (departing from the practices of previous superintendents). He had few informal contacts with his staff, turning down all social invitations except those of a few associates. He interposed an executive secretary between himself and the staff for the handling of all organizational matters. He resided in the farthest outskirts of Midland. He vacationed in Wisconsin. With some oversimplification, it could be said he had few ties with Midland and he sought none.

This self-imposed isolation was entirely congruent with an image of himself which he valued highly. The image was of the remote leader—above the fray, detached from personal involvement, charismatic, selfless. He read avidly Richard Neustadt's Machiavellian picture of the American presidency, *Presidential Power,*[2] in which the successful president is portrayed as a man who understands how to manipulate followers, who obtains cooperation by genius and gall. That the president was both the head and the heart of the polity was immensely appealing. Leadership was the concept he most frequently mentioned, by which he meant articulate dramatization ("I'm a sucker for quotations"), imposition of one's convictions ("You don't equivocate"), and personal responsibility ("[I] must assume those obligations of being the executive"). The staff was to do his bidding, and if arm twisting and casuistry were necessary to prevail, so be it. The staff was an unavoidable bottleneck in the production of independent-minded schoolchildren.

Organizational accomplishments became personal achievements. "I am very proud of this Board," he stated in a proprietary way, as if the board members who had appointed him had really been his personal selections. He was the executive of the outfit; he *was* the school system. He had no respect for the qualms and shortcomings of his staff. He

[2] Richard Neustadt, *Presidential Power* (New York: John Wiley & Sons, 1960).

looked on doubting Thomases around him as personally encumbering; they were to be eliminated, just as he might have scourged his own personal misgivings. Once he committed himself to a course of action, the more intense the staff's misgivings came to be, the more illegitimate those doubts appeared.

Bartkowicz was a man of articulateness and accomplishment; and every accomplishment fed his self-confidence and zeal. He was convinced that action was always better than inaction. Initiatives were his contribution to his organization, and (he might well have echoed Neustadt's remark about the presidency) "initiatives are what they want."[3]

Miss O'Hara, the associate superintendent, was in her late sixties. She had spent forty-six years in the Midland system, rising through the ranks from teacher to principal to superintendent. She was soft-spoken, but her words were measured to fit a sophisticated and highly detailed mental frame of reference.

She had been born into an immigrant family which valued education and the Catholic religion. She had come through Midland parochial and public schools and eventually Teachers' College. She had an apartment in the heart of downtown Midland. Her anchor was Midland and its educational system. Her friends were almost entirely school teachers. She was a member of all the system's social organizations and practically every professional association. She contributed her energies to community causes of every variety—family services, foundling homes, social welfare programs—which she enjoyed for the opportunity to work with "influential lawyers and business people, and women, social women, with time, but quite high up." She was fond of the big and small of Midland.

She harbored an acute ambivalence about administrative work. She enjoyed working with the community elite; but "if I had my choice, the pleasantest, most rewarding job is being principal of an elementary school, a small one, say about four hundred children." She fought her isolation. Isolation did not fit her image of what a leader should be. A leader in her view, was a message center, "the channel of communication between the board and the staff."[4] It was her job to translate

[3] *Ibid.*, p. 7.

[4] These words are Miss O'Hara's, but Chester I. Barnard has emphasized the same point in a famous passage: "For the function of the center of communication in an organization is to translate the incoming communications concerning external conditions, the progress of activity, successes, failures,

incoming messages, sending them along to others in the organization in more understandable and operational form. As a superintendent she was obliged to understand the deep feelings implicit in those messages from the board and the staff. In the translation process, a leader's task was to resolve emotional and ethical conflicts resulting from the collision of organizational and personal obligations. She did not view herself as the initiative giver; initiatives came from those closest to the problems ("Right now I am further away than I was as a first-grade teacher, and I get more ineffective"). Her job was creating morale, of pulling the group together for a start and then helping the staff derive a sense of self-esteem from its involvement in the Midland school system. As a leader she was obliged to help her staff be happy in their work. The more intense their misgivings, the greater her obligation to understand and accommodate those feelings.

In obvious contrast to Bartkowicz's concepts, leadership was a transaction not a command, and influential communication a dialogue not a soliloquy. Power was based on calling up credits due a leader who had served a follower in a previous instance; it was not human manipulation. Her idea of good leadership was not that of Dr. Bartkowicz or even of the late President Kennedy (as Neustadt might have pictured him), but of Rizzuto, the school board chairman. In talking of the prayer ban, Miss O'Hara remarked;

> It was only due to Vince Rizzuto's good leadership that it didn't really all blow up. He was influential, almost entirely on a personal contact basis . . . [His] social contacts are rooted in the middle-class teacher group, and I know there was a lot of respect for the way he accepted the decision. The staff seemed to say, if Vince Rizzuto accepts it, we can accept it.

In short, as she saw matters, the voluntary effort of the teachers was the indispensable unit of the school system: leadership was to make it possible for the teacher to get supportive materials, skills, confidence, and information from and to other teachers and the school board. The

---

difficulties, dangers, into outgoing communications in terms of new activities, preparatory steps, etc., all shaped according to the ultimate as well as the intermediate purposes to be served. There is accordingly required more or less mastery of the technologies involved, of the capabilities of personnel, of the subsidiary organizations, of the principles of action relative to purpose, of the interpretation of environmental factors, and a power of discrimination . . ." *The Functions of the Executive* (Cambridge, Mass.: Harvard University Press, 1938), p. 178.

impact on the child came from a teacher's behavior in class. And while the staff could be ordered about, each demand, if it appeared unjustified, increased hostility and affected "the manner in which they taught." Ultimately, when the extremely difficult situation arose, the commands would be ineffectual—that is, the staff would rebel.

Miss O'Hara's view of power as transaction was not the only departure she made from Dr. Bartkowicz. Where Bartkowicz viewed organizational achievements as his personal achievements, Miss O'Hara, without being falsely modest, discounted her personal contributions. She was proud of "our board," not because it accepted her advice, but because it came to grips with the moral conflicts within the hearts of the staff. Her sense of self-esteem stemmed from her identification with the system: she did not want to separate her contribution from the staff's contribution. When she talked about her own work, she talked about "we."

To sharpen the contrast, we might say that Miss O'Hara felt a responsibility to those in her organization; Bartkowicz felt obliged to make his organization live up to some vague code of public responsibilities. Each derived satisfaction from the role of leader, but the acts of leadership which swelled Bartkowicz's self-esteem would have shamed Miss O'Hara; conversely, the kind of leadership which made Miss O'Hara proudest would have appeared a shortcoming to Bartkowicz. In his frame of reference, his greatest worry was inertia; in hers, it was insurrection.

The Principals

Of the nineteen principals interviewed for this study, fifteen had charge of elementary schools, two of junior highs, and two of senior highs. The modal principal was a woman (ten, of whom eight were spinsters), Roman Catholic (fourteen), middle of the road in domestic politics (nine), politically unaffiliated (fifteen), and a native Midland citizen (seventeen). Even more striking, the modal term of service as a teacher and administrator in the Midland school system exceeded thirty years. None had served less than ten years. There was no lateral entry into a principalship in Midland. The women and men who became principals had invariably received their apprenticeship in Midland public schools. The only reality they knew was Midland.

Well over half had had administrative jobs as supervisors and principals for a decade or more. Among the female principals, a fair measure of informal interchange took place. The male principals, more jealous of their status and more competitive with each other, shared little in the way of friendship. In the interviews derogatory remarks about their confreres slipped from the men's lips. Woodford, a principal, confirmed the impression: "None of the [male] principals work really as a community."

Much of the information about the Midland school system came to the principals by way of staff meetings and an informal association called the Principals' Club. The interviews, however, revealed one other—curious—source. It was the problem child: the Jehovah's Witness; the Negro boy whose mother was a prostitute; the Jewish boy with the intensely Orthodox family; the child of disturbed parents; a "real smart boy" who wrote caustic editorials in the newspaper. The problem child was the single automatic source of information available to the principal; knowledge of him came as an incidental by-product of the principal's most time-consuming job: dealing with the atypical case. Automatic information for the principal was invariably pathological. Conscious attempts to adjust for this bias of the available helped to overcome the bleak picture of a generation "going to Hell in a handbasket," but to do so a principal had to be aware of the dangers of passive reception of the reality around her.

Miss Barrone and Miss FitzGerald

Let us look at two of these principals in detail, paying attention to their methods of learning about what went on. Miss Barrone and Miss FitzGerald had both taught in the system for more than twenty-five years. Both had been educated in Midland public schools. Both had enjoyed teaching, and both periodically longed to get back in the classrooms. Both participated in the Principals' Club to a great extent. Both were devout Roman Catholics. Neither was a liberal politically, Miss Barrone being conservative domestically and Miss FitzGerald a middle-of-the-roader. Most importantly for the present discussion, both were principals in schools where the population was religiously mixed. What kind of perceptual habits did these two women have? What kind of questions did they put to the political and educational reality all about them?

Miss Barrone was the principal of a mixed Catholic-Negro school. She was small, standing barely five feet high. During the interviews her eyes shone from behind extruded eyelids, giving her Italian face a vivacity and keenness which were notable.

As I got acquainted with Miss Barrone, I soon came to know about her family: her parents and brothers and sisters. She spoke of her childhood with pride. She told me of her immigrant parents and of their people back it Italy. She detailed how her seven brothers and sisters had been brought up and how they had played pranks on each other. She told me what her family was doing now. Her analogies were drawn from her family experience, and her colloquies were punctuated with quotes from her father. Her family was her psychological anchor.

Her childhood memories were deep and warm and joyful. Guiding her own behavior were the patterns she had observed in her parents' lives. One characteristic of the old Barrone home had been discussion.

> Ours was a political home. We were first-generation Italian. My father was particularly interested in politics. I can remember groups of my father's friends in to discuss news items. There were quite heated discussions about problems in this country as they affected their homeland, about labor, prevailing prices, and bringing up children. The house wasn't that big; so we couldn't help hearing. And my father taught me about politics.

Her childhood education in politics had given her a capital of facts and concepts which served her well even to the present. One might almost have said she commanded a natural background of information about the political system. Political concepts had meaning to her. Each of her abstractions was followed by a specific illustration, sometimes homely, sometimes elegant. In talking about the Supreme Court, she could say its function was to "balance the individual welfare against the general welfare. . . . Heck, in my family there were eight brothers and sisters. I really had to fight for my rights. It made for a climate of general welfare."

Her background had provided her the tools necessary to make sense of politics. She knew, almost instinctively, what political facts were crucial and worth looking at.

With this inheritance, politics and politicians were never a mystery. Men in political life were well meaning, even benevolent. Of the Supreme Court justices, for example, Miss Barrone thought they were "like me with the boys and girls: I may scold them once in a while, but underneath they know I love them." Men of politics loved their citizenry.

Politicians could be mistaken sometimes, but they were not malicious. As Miss Barrone understood political life, the politician's shortcomings resulted from the difficulties of getting crucial information.

"Not getting the word from all the points of need" caused mistakes. Conversely, successful decision makers were those who understood how elusive information was. One must research—look anew at—familiar situations for non-obvious factors. Miss Barrone imposed on herself the obligation to keep her mind open to hard-to-see information, and she obliged herself to do it continuously. "As an administrator I knew that there comes a time when you have to take a stand"; and unless she was constantly looking for the other sides of events, she might be caught short when a crucial decision was forced on her.

As part of this continuing research of the world, she chose to live with her brothers and sisters because the interests of school personnel were not extended enough. "Extended" was the word for her family: teacher, factory supervisor, salesman, librarian, pharmacist, professor, and office manager. Miss Barrone, it is easy to imagine, planted herself in the midst of those continuing family discussions, testing out ideas and filling her mind with information hard to get in the less extended sphere of the Midland school system.

To this active gatherer of information—this person who explained political phenomena in terms of the availability of accurate information—the Supreme Court seemed, of all political bodies, the most intellectual and the most open. When she was confronted by the *Schempp* decision which prohibited her beloved religious devotionals, she was shocked at herself because "I did not decide the way they did." She was not indignant at the Court but upset with herself. The Court, as a body of men in politics, established par for the political course, and she had not met it. She was rudely awakened by her failure to guess correctly. Had she failed to do her homework? Had she failed to keep her mind and eyes open to the real world? And off she went to research her school, to look with new eyes at those dozen classrooms which she had overconfidently thought she knew so well, marching into each classroom in the proud intellectual traditions of her ancestors, of her mother's and father's people.

Put Miss FitzGerald beside Miss Barrone. She was a principal in a mixed Catholic-Jewish elementary school. She was tall, soft-spoken, a little shy, attractive. She was a spinster who lived with her two sisters, both of whom were teachers. Miss FitzGerald had an active social life, being state president of an honorary society and devoting great efforts to church groups.

I could have talked all day with Miss FitzGerald before she would have mentioned her family. Her childhood memories were negative memories, lifeless memories. Her adult life was working against the grain of her childhood. She was reacting against that which had been specific and intimate, in sharp contrast to Miss Barrone's responsiveness to her family traditions.

Unlike Miss Barrone, Miss FitzGerald had no political or cultural inheritance. She had no childhood capital of facts and concepts to employ in making sense of the real world. Without these natural resources she had had to be a self-made woman, creating her own intellectual tools. For example, Miss Barrone's rich political education at her father's knee contrasted sharply with Miss FitzGerald's anemic book learning. ("In the courses on leadership I took, I learned that the people who are going to be involved should be in on the organization of the plans.") All that she knew of politics, and of other realms, had been consciously and painfully assimilated. Nothing had come naturally.

With an impoverished frame of reference to make sense of real-world complexities, without an intellectual traffic cop to tell her where data fitted, Miss FitzGerald had found political reality (and other realities) overwhelming. Every complication had been a disaster.

At some point in Miss FitzGerald's life she had come upon an island of safety: the Church. It had provided her a picture of reality which gave a context to some of her perceptions. She had clung to that island, and she had attempted thereafter to avoid the disasters of new complications. The polity, as a major source of incongruent messages, now loomed as an adversary, bombarding the people (that is, Miss FitzGerald) with alien and incomprehensible ideas.

Because she felt she had to maintain the world much as she had seen it long ago, she now set herself in a comfortable social milieu and passively received the available information. With old and like-minded acquaintances, she found she got reenforcement for what she already knew. Unlike Miss Barrone, who purposefully set out to extend her sphere, Miss FitzGerald did just the opposite, saying: "You kind of favor those people you are talking to for other reasons; then you say, come over for dinner." Miss FitzGerald would "kind of favor" people who did not upset a world she found hard to understand.

When the prayer ban was put into effect, she reacted as if she were personally threatened. She attended the administrator's meeting where, according to her account, the details of the school board rule were explained and justified by Goldman. "We were told what we would have to do . . . It was something I wrote down in a notebook and that

I told the teachers in turn." Then, one infers, she dropped the notes into the trash and departed, retreating to her honorary society where, as one of her colleagues put it, "They choose a kind of people who would not be dissenters." In that sanctuary she regained her poise.

Berman, the Jewish junior high school principal, clutched at a version of reality with a ferocity equal to Miss FitzGerald's desperation. The first Jew to obtain a school principalship, Berman had been ravaged by his rise to the top. He suffered severe asthmatic and sinus attacks; he was susceptible to numerous small illnesses. Orphaned as a child, raised by his Jewish grandmother in the Jewish ghetto of Midland, he eschewed Jewish groups. Berman had overreacted in accepting Gentile sentiment, and in this way had lost the respect of Jews. Since he also distrusted Catholics ("Give them a foot, and they want forty-four yards") and Negroes ("They are all for personal aggrandizement"), he was culturally isolated. To bear this solitude, he committed himself to an almost paranoiac view of the world in which he was the victim. To sustain this view, he had had to blind himself to the case for the opposition: Jewish aspirations, minority groups' problems, blue-collar demands. As he put it, "My decision maker is myself," and he was in a fight against the "hypocrites—the freethinkers." Berman was indentured to a view of the universe, to which he had entrusted his birthright. The point is that Berman's vicious world view was reenforced by the bleak stories invariably told by students in trouble. He—and Miss FitzGerald too—had no incentive to expose themselves actively to other realities, for their own outlooks had no room for optimism.

In Midland's school system there were few individuals with such fervent strangleholds on a version of reality. Most officials resembled Miss Barrone in her active curiosity. The majority had its "door open," its "ear to the ground." Its perceptual habits were healthy, not morbid.

Summary

Each of the twenty-eight respondents who comprised this study had his own public, his own set of self-expectations, and his own perceptual habits. Whom they were conforming to, what kinds of self-images they aspired to, what commitments they had to specific versions of reality —all were highly variable, even within a single system, situated in a single locality.

When law impinges on the mental frames of a variety of individuals, emphasizing different values and implying discrepant realities, the repercussions may be very different depending on these variabilities.

The same law may bolster one person's estimate of himself and subvert another's, may make one man's world a leaky ship and the other's intellectually exciting, may make one person a hero to his friends and the other a bum to his. Alexander Leighton, in his seminal study of the imprisonment of the Japanese-Americans during World War II, wrote:

> Because systems of belief have deep connection with the springs of men's existence, they are often interdependent in a manner that may not be obvious on the surface. The theory of organic evolution had bearing on morals because both morals and the conception of the origin of the species are encompassed by beliefs called the Christian religion. Systems of belief resemble a thick matting of roots under the floor of the forest which if cut may result in the withering of some distant bush or a whole tree. The man who intrudes into another culture, or way of life, with administrative acts may be like one who cuts bothersome roots without being aware of their functions and interconnections . . . The people of the other culture, however, like the trees of the forest, even if sometimes ignorant of the functional nature of their systems of belief, nevertheless feel it when their roots are cut.[5]

Law acting on Midland citizens, like American administrative measures working on the Japanese belief systems, was likely to have unexpected (and unwanted) psychological repercussions. We would expect a reaction, sometimes intense, to follow unless these repercussions could be anticipated and mitigated. Attitudes inconsistent with the law had to be cut out of the individual's frame of reference to make way for new feelings and beliefs, but the cutting had to be done without withering his self-esteem or his chances of enjoying old friendships or his self-confidence. To make these delicate fittings for large numbers of people was a monumental task, manageable only because under the appropriate conditions these fittings could be done disjointedly, in an infinite number of informal seminars in a social process. I shall eventually detail how these cuttings were made in Midland, among Midland educators, but first I must describe the original attitudes of Midland officialdom. How did they feel about schoolhouse religion before the *Schempp* case?

[5] Alexander H. Leighton, *The Governing of Men* (Princeton: Princeton University Press, 1946), pp. 291-92.

IV

Original Attitudes toward Schoolhouse Religion

The Consensus on Ethical Principles

If you were to have asked a Midland educator before *Schempp* how he ought to behave toward the schoolchildren in his custody, the probabilities would have been very great that he would have responded in one of two ways: either, "I ought to help my students," or, "I should refrain from hurting them." Were you to have talked longer, he would probably have voiced both these norms. Giving help and avoiding hurt were the ways Midland educators conceived their duties.[1]

One might well have expected him to have answered your question in a different way. He might have said: "Treat all the children equally," or, "Cram their heads full of concepts and facts," or, "Keep the kids off the streets," or, "Make them good citizens," or, "Put the fear of God in them," or, "Drive the mischief out of them." It is true that equal treatment, to take one example, might have been less likely to hurt a class of schoolchildren than its opposite of discrimination, yet the equality principle was very different from the "do not hurt" and "help" doctrines. Not hurting and helping required adaptation to the student's individual circumstances. Under some conditions discriminating treatment might have been necessary to help an individual student and equal treatment might have hurt him. In that case the equality principle would have been incompatible with the ethics of Midland educators. Underlying the Midland administrator's concept of his pro-

[1] The discussion in this and the next chapter is based exclusively on the results of the first interview, conducted in early 1963, several months before the Supreme Court decided *Schempp*.

fessional obligation was his responsibility to detect each child's individuality and tailor an education to it. In the perspective of the norms not chosen, this ethical unanimity on giving help and avoiding hurt was remarkable.

Individual officials varied in the priority which they gave to one or the other of these two rules. Two principals, Rynne and Russo, represented the extremes.

James Rynne, at forty-five, was ten years older than Frank Russo. He had thirteen years of administrative experience as assistant principal and later as principal of a junior high school, Russo had but one year as principal of an elementary school. In some respects, however, there was a resemblance between the two men. Rynne was president of the teachers' association, the independent labor organization representing 80 per cent of the staff, and Russo was his first vice-president and likely successor. Both were politically middle-of-the-road. Both were Catholics. Both were principals of schools in homogeneously Catholic neighborhoods. Both were young men on the make in a school system undergoing drastic remodernizing.

Rynne, however, was much less aggressive than Russo, much the more conciliatory of the two men. His very physical features seemed to bespeak this conciliatory streak. Although once a fine athlete, his sizable anatomy now bulged indulgently. He smiled jovially, welcomed strangers warmly, and disliked dispute. Within the limits allowed to a regular guy, Rynne believed that the better part of valor was discretion. He hated the thought of injury or of injurious thoughts. During the interview he several times seemed to wince when he recalled certain events: American treatment of Japanese war prisoners, a defense lawyer's interrogation of a policeman on the witness stand, several teachers who "ride roughshod over their kids."

He saw himself as a conciliator, invariably trying to get around bitterness and to "avoid what we differ on." During the interview he proudly mentioned mediating disputes in the teachers' association, in the community, and on the athletic field. Even in the interview he mediated every difficult question, and the interview lasted two hours longer than average.

Now it was quite plain that Rynne tended to superordinate the ethical norm, "Do not hurt," over any other consideration. In discussing schoolhouse religion, he saw that any change in the status quo would "take some things away from" the people, yet at the same time he conceded that a prayer ban was an attempt to stop any bitterness. When asked to predict whether certain religious practices in the public schools would be constitutional, he agonized over each question until he happened on the idea of legal compulsion as being the constitutionally objectionable factor. Thereafter, anything which offered a legal option to the student to avoid hurt by being silent or not attending he deemed constitutional. Not once did he mention the possibility of improving students. Avoiding fights, hatred, bitterness, and domineering was his credo. If a practice did not hurt someone, then it was "O.K."

Frank Russo, on the other hand, had a lean look. Assertive, aggressive, and brash, he placed the improvement of each of his students at the top of his agenda. If he did not help students who happened to come within his influence, he felt he had failed them. He was "their golden boy. In their eyes I can do no wrong."

His goal was to use his goodwill to influence boys and girls for good, to make them better, to add to the puny resources they brought from home. The child had to have the teacher's help to fill the void left by the parents' neglect. The teacher, while he had to protect the unusual children from hazing, was obliged to help familiarize them with normal practices—for example, to teach the Jehovah's Witness children how to salute the flag. In Russo's view of himself, merely to refrain from hurting a student was an insufficient rule of conduct when teachers, with a little effort, could exercise such tremendous grassroots influence.

Most officials had fuzzier priorities in the matter of these ethical principles than Rynne or Russo. They agreed that "No one has a right to hurt a child," yet at the same time they doubted that a teacher's neutrality in a child's education was either possible or desirable.

Two ethical principles converged on the public schools in Midland, each seeking to extend its dominion over treatment of students. Sometimes one seemed better; at another moment the second seemed more appropriate. But, more often than not, the choice was dreadfully ambiguous. For an administrator, charged with formulating general programs, the alternative principles presented a Hobson's choice: Was it better to give help to all but risk the danger of hurting a few, or to refrain from injury and run the risk of neglecting all?

What did the concepts of hurt and help mean in practice? They pertained to the never ending collisions between educators and parents. When a Midland educator said the school had hurt a child, he was asserting that a teacher had deflected the parent's influence in a situation where such deflection was ill-advised. Conversely, when he believed that the parent's influence had been properly overridden, he would remark that the child had been helped. An administrator like Rynne, who said, "I shall not hurt my students," was really concluding that parents had charge of their children's destiny, and their wishes were entitled to be his command. An administrator like Russo, on the other hand, was convinced that parents exercised a baleful impact; hence, for him it was legitimate to ignore parents. In short, hurt and help were ethical euphemisms in Midland school administration. The phrases summed up conclusions. If an official had decided to oppose, modify, or refute the values, expectations, demands, ethics, or religion which the child brought from home, he saw himself as conforming to the "help" principle. If, on the other hand, he had decided that parents were likely to act more correctly, legitimately, carefully, or harmlessly than himself in a child's life, he summed up his conclusions in the "Do not hurt" norm.

Two board members—the Jewish lawyer Goldman and the Negro social worker Coleman—had opposed positions on this matter of parental demands, and their positions epitomized a part of the American history of their own minority groups. For Goldman, the proper way for educators to behave was to use self-restraint. Only in curriculum matters was the school official to tamper with the parents' demands for their children; in other areas, hands off, laissez faire, was the rule. According to Goldman, the home ought to be the anchor for the Jewish child; the rich cultural traditions of the Jewish family provided sufficient knowledge and social skills to make the child an asset to American society, to give the child a basis for acceptance as an American. Conflict between the home and the school, however, caused the Jewish child to doubt his Americanism; Goldman put it nicely: "It's hard for Jewish kids outside of New York to have a sense of identity."

Not so for Coleman, the son of a Negro laborer with a third grade education. The more the differences between the backgrounds of Negro and white children were eliminated, the more the Negro became Americanized. Coleman believed that the Negro home tended to starve the child of the acceptable cultural traditions and practices necessary to assimilate him into American life, thereby depriving the child of his chance to be an American. Until the inhibiting influence of the ignorant Negro parent could be wiped away, the Negro child would remain apart from his community. In detailing two incidents, Coleman revealed his childhood need of confirming his identity as an American.

I can remember saluting the flag—a lot of ritual cropped up during World War II. I guess, during the thirties, we were so glad to get food that we didn't pay much attention to ceremony. When our country was threatened, we straightened up and paid attention to ritual. What I really remember—and maybe this will tell a lot about me—I was thirteen or fourteen before I learned a blessing. My uncle taught me one, and I have never forgotten it. Prayer is just a ritual . . ."

A commonly shared ritual was the indicia of Americanism.

As Coleman saw the history of his race, World War II had raised the status of Negroes. For the first time they were no longer considered a social problem but accepted as indispensable contributors to the national effort. The measure of their acceptance was inclusion in the ritual of pledging allegiance to the flag. Instruction in this ritual made them citizens, like the whites, and allowed them to escape the stigma of being Negro. Coleman, however, learned prayers so late in his adolescence that he experienced being left out of a fundamental American ceremony. He was an outsider for not knowing what white children knew. This social isolation was "what I really remember."

Coleman was far more activist in his expectations of the school system than was Goldman. Goldman wanted laissez faire, wanted the schools to cease putting Jewish children outside the American traditions. Coleman wanted help, wanted the schools to make Negroes American. Both these men emphasized the collision between parent and educator in guiding the child's destiny. The conflict was agonizing, perpetual, and universally recognized. In which direction the individual official was likely to resolve each struggle turned on personality, personal experience, and the educational circumstances.

Consensus on Application of the Ethical Principles

I have said that educators had to make general policies in the light of ethical principles which obliged them to recognize the individuality of each student. Thereby resulted their dilemma: to hurt a few, or to neglect all. In coming to grips with this quandary, Midland educators made distinctions between circumstances in which the "help" principle (and its policy consequence, "hurt a few") applied and those in which the "do not hurt" principle (and its policy corollary, "neglect all") was more appropriate.

There was a high degree of agreement on the application of the "help" principle in three aspects of the student's life. The school system could override the parents in respect of the student's medical treatment (which included oral vaccines and psychiatric help but not sex education), the substance of his curriculum (for instance, no parent could rightfully object to a course concerning totalitarianism), and his learning of the American heritage (patriotism). In these three areas parental demands were universally regarded as illegitimate.

Near unanimity could be found about a fourth area: the realm of character. Goldman tended to be suspicious of the school's right to influence children's morals, but he was alone. The feeling was overwhelming that an educator was obliged to better the character of students. Whether a child's character developed for good or ill was the educator's responsibility; the student's moral growth provided the educator his greatest satisfactions.

In the realm of character, the Midland educator viewed himself as having a duty to help the child transcend his family background: he had to assist the child to develop strength, tolerance, a sense of what was important, manners, respect, a sense of values, sympathetic understanding,—in short, morals; the child had to be diverted from materialism, selfishness, anger, and lawlessness. Make no mistake about it: to withhold needed help in the area of character training was a shortcoming of the gravest nature. The reluctant educator failed the child. Miss FitzGerald, in her doctrinaire way, exaggerated the point but thereby clarified it when she said that children who did not develop fully were "a criticism of ourselves and how they have been taught."

Religious Development

The question of the child's religious development shattered the consensus on application of the ethical principles. At least eight of the twenty-eight officials in the original interview felt that the religious training of the child was the business of educators, who could properly divert the child's spiritual development in constructive ways. For the others, the "do not hurt" imperative was paramount. An educator acted improperly if he overrode the family's religious heritage. But in its concrete application, this "do not hurt" norm raised a further question: did non-interference require the school to become a place where children could practice their various familial religions if they wished, or did it mean that schools were completely out of bounds for any spiritual practices? Those who felt that schools should be an exercise ground for inherited religious practices have to be distinguished from those officials who thought the doors should be barred even to religious calisthenics.

The consensus shattered, then, into three parts. Let us look at three principals who, in some way, illustrated the various fragments of this discord: Berman, a junior high school principal; and Kaplan and Farley, two of the elementary school principals.

Harold Berman held a view that he had to help the student in his spiritual growth. Berman was, as I said in the preceding chapter, culturally isolated, a man without a community, serving a community which did not appreciate him. In facing up to his rejection, it was crucial to his self-esteem that the people rejecting him were stupid, jaundiced, perverted. Furthermore, he saw himself as the isolated, intellectual aristocrat, ministering to the sons and daughters of the hoi polloi and freeing them from the bondages of their parents.

The task of the educator was to save the child, in all phases of his development, from the neglect, crudity, and emptiness of family life. The teacher stood *in loco parentis,* taking over the perquisites and privileges of parenthood. If the educator failed in this gigantic task, "this country will fall apart at the seams."

One of the perquisites was the right to guide the citizenry's "practically heathen" children in their spiritual development. Religion (to know God) was a precondition to knowing how to live and was necessary to the task of rearming the world in morals.

Isaiah Kaplan espoused a view directly opposed to Berman's. He believed that the schools had no business tampering with a student's religious beliefs. Kaplan, who taught twenty-seven years before receiving his appointment as principal in an elementary school in well-to-do Forest Hill, was a devout Jew, exhibiting his Hebraic scholarship proudly and cherishing his synagogue-community life. He began his interview with the statement, "I am a cynic", and ended it by saying, "It's a wonderful world to be at work in." He tended first to state his pessimism, to look for subtle insults, and to enjoy a sense of persecution. Generally, his optimism would surface, however, with the result that his intellect might first seem to be inconsistent and his behavior erratic. To the contrary, he was in fact a man of both sad and joyful aspect, who was saved from contradictory expectations by a subtle set of distinctions and qualifications within a sophisticated frame of reference.

He had suffered ignominy as a result of his Judaism and his archetypal Semitic face. The deep hurt of his experience burst out as we closed the interview.

In 1929, I remember taking my master's examination in English. The exam had been originally scheduled for Saturday, and for us Jews it fell on a religious holiday. Eventually, we went to the administration to get a special examination to be given all of us the following Monday. On Monday all the Jewish kids were taking the exam, when the teacher, a well-known scholar, came in and said, "I don't know what all you Semites are doing, taking this English exam." He was a very prejudiced man, I still think he was a great scholar, but he was a poor man.

At some time since 1929, Kaplan rejected the hostile opinion of this "great scholar." Kaplan did not turn hate in on himself because admirable men were derogatory toward him. He had survived the crushing affront (and others like it) by differentiating between scholarship and manliness, between the various areas in which admirable men were expert and should be influential and those which were a matter of private concern. There was an area of personal development that was all the individual's own responsibility, a citadel of privacy above reproach and into which no person—teacher or friend—could tread.

The differentiation between private and public, inviolate and susceptible, structured Kaplan's view of reality. He made sense of the events of the day as aspects of the unending struggle between the individual, with his undefilable citadel, on the one hand, and the supersolicitous and officious, on the other. Where Berman condemned families for their neglect of their children's religious development, Kaplan remarked that families were overbearing, putting pressure on the school system "to propound their own point of view" to the children in families other than their own. Schoolhouse religion invaded the little seed of integrity which was the child's and his family's own preserve. Religion, being neither a necessary nor sufficient condition to being a good man, was outside the admittedly proper moral concern of educators.

Paul Farley agreed with Kaplan that the schools should not meddle with the religious heritage of the individual student, but he applied this belief in a very different manner. Farley had been born and had lived his entire life within a half-mile radius of the elementary school he administered. He envisioned himself more the cigar-smoking Irish politician than the educator—the sheer office walls of the old school seemed to cabin and frustrate him.

He had run for mayor of Midland a few years before and after his defeat had formed his own (minuscule) independent party, flyspecking from one crisis to another, and breaking into the newspapers every fortnight. He enjoyed being popular; what he liked most was the prestige of being a broker of community affairs. He was what he thought he ought to be: a politician, with the instincts for service and the susceptibilities for gratitude which politicians distinctively display. He thought of himself as part of an organic Irish neighborhood, an insider, a public servant of the community and for the community.

Farley fitted his job as principal into this public servant framework. He was there to serve the parent not the student. He was charged with the duty of keeping the kids off the streets until the parents got home from work—a kind of pubescent day nursery.

As a trustee of the children for the parents, he had limited powers; he was not a substitute for a father. His job was to encourage the child's congenital attitudes, to nourish the manners, interests, ethics, religion, tastes, world views, and ideas his parents gave him.

Farley would not have wanted the schools to override the parents; that was a breach of his fiduciary obligation. But neither would he have left the environment neutral, as Kaplan would have it. Farley would say: "A kid has fear and respect for his religion, which he gets in his home. In school if there was no religion, he might lose that fear and respect." Since a "kid" was inclined to regard whatever was omitted from school as unimportant, Kaplan's kind of secular neutrality worked to cast doubt upon the family sectarianism.

Farley, always the politician, looking for ways to serve his constituency as it wished to be served, hated to waste his opportunities to help out. His job was to accommodate everyone. The school could be used as a public exercise ground where each child could practice the learning obtained in the home. If such learning helped the parents in teaching the kid some morals, then all the more reason was there for making the schoolroom a home away from home.

Berman, Kaplan, Farley—these three men resembled each other and the rest of the Midland officials by virtue of the fact that their original predispositions about schoolhouse religion were psychologically consistent with what we know of their self-images, with their reality views, and with the rest of their attitudes. In none of these three men was there much psychological tension involved in the holding of their various views. All were emotionally and intellectually at ease before the prayer cases.

Characterizing the Practice

One further point: my conclusions were that about half the educators agreed with Kaplan that sectarian religious development was out of bounds. In situations where the student's character development was involved, parental practices might be tampered with; but where his religious development was involved, the family inheritance was inviolable. This consensus was not without difficulty in its application. The problem arose in characterizing whether a particular practice was one of morals or faith.

Was a Hallowe'en party a practice involving a child's character or his religion? The religious practice of the children of some Jehovah's Witnesses forbade participation in frivolity. Was celebrating Hallowe'en a religious practice and therefore taboo in a public school? Miss Barrone, for all the educators, answered no. In talking about her treatment of the Jehovah's Witness children, she observed:

It can reach so many places—this matter of religion. It has a lot of ramifications. Sometimes (I'm probably wrong to step in), I sometimes tell those children, "If something is not seriously bad and if you believe in your heart in God, remember He's made joy as much as sorrow," and I try to get them to join in with the other children. With kids brought up in this strict religion where they are not allowed to enjoy themselves, they can become problematical and emotional children.

The causal connection between religion and morality was so insistent that characterizing ceremonies as if they involved one and not the other became close to impossible. If Miss Barrone abstained from interfering with the parents' control of the child's religious training, then the child was likely to become so constricted in his emotional, medical, and social condition that he could not become a good citizen. The solution to the dilemma of Miss Barrone and the others who believed that the religious citadel was inviolable was to forget that a Hallowe'en party had any religious significance and to regard it exclusively in terms of its socializing aspects. Miss Barrone found the distinction a legitimate one because she intended the party only to have a social purpose.

In a similar way a number of officials thought of the saying of the Lord's Prayer or the singing of Christmas carols not as a religious exercise but as a character-building routine. They secularized these practices, dissociating them from sectarian religion and making them part of a civic heritage. Typically, Bartkowicz intended this religiously derived part of the civic heritage only as a means to "teach right and wrong—and justice, respect for property, everything . . . What's important about religion are the common ethical principles." These common, everyday religious ceremonies were heard in stores and on television variety shows. The purpose of school officials in permitting this kind of religion was to use it as the handmaiden of the state, to teach good citizenship. In light of the teacher's purpose, the saying of the Lord's Prayer or the singing of carols did not fall within the injunction against meddling with religious values.

The Four Self-Images

In reviewing the content of the interviews, I thought that four quite distinct types of attitudes could be detected among the educators' belief systems. I should warn the reader that what follows is an analysis of the data based on my own impressions; the written interviews were not reviewed by a third party to check any bias in my own interpretation of the data. Nor did I establish any hard-and-fast quantification rules against which I could check my inclinations.

With that reservation understood, we can summarize the four different self-images within the Midland system in terms of the responsibility of the public school official for the spiritual growth of students. First, there was the belief that the teacher was obliged to take a hand in the students' religious development. Linked with this policy was the factual presupposition that religion was necessary and sufficient to create good character: "It is the fear of God that makes a person a person." An atheist could not be a good citizen because religious conviction was a precondition of ethics. In this attitude any sectarian differences among formal religious institutions were ignored. This band of concepts and cognitions we shall call the unionist self-image, to express the union between religion and character.

On the school board, chairman Rizzuto and the pediatrician Clancy shared this attitude. Among the principals, Berman, Russo, and Miss FitzGerald held similar beliefs, as did three others: Mareno, a senior high principal who was a militant and devout Roman Catholic; the gentle Miss Molly O'Brien; and Miss Barber, a friend of Miss FitzGerald and her associate in the honorary society.

A second self-image prohibited tampering with a child's congenital faith but at the same time obliged the school official to provide a minimal amount of bolstering of the religious beliefs which the child brought from his home. Tied in with this norm was the fact that religion was not essential but was sufficient to produce good character. For example, the atheist was not necessarily a bad man, but he was more likely to be worse than the person who belonged to a sectarian organization. We shall call this self-image that of the trustee, to indicate the fiduciary relationship extending from the educator to the parents. It might be summed up by the statement that religion is all right in the schools if the families do not object.

Farley was a trustee, as was Rynne. So was Cagney, who, like Farley, lived within the neighborhood his school served, the middle-class, home-owning, suburb-like Irish community Williamstown.

A third self-image emphasized that in sectarian matters a teacher had to be neutral. At the same time a few conventional and uniform religiously derived rituals were deemed to be character building not religious. The cognition frequently involved in this self-image was the certitude that collective pageantry and ceremony of any sort was necessary (but not sufficient) to knit a student body together. This set of beliefs, epitomized by the remark, "There is nothing wrong with a simple prayer," we shall call the patriot self-image, because it highlighted the civic rather than the religious aspect of devotional exercises.

Miss O'Hara, Dr. Bartkowicz, and Miss Barrone shared this self-image of the patriot with four other principals: the senior high school principal Murphy; the articulate and hard-working Reform Jew Mrs. Goldberg; and two political liberals, Miss Mercer and Mrs. Toreno.

A fourth group of persons made a sharp distinction between those practices which had a religious overtone from those which did not ("If it were of a religious nature, it should not be in the schools at all"). The related cognitions were that any religious practice was sectarian, and sectarianism as taught in the public schools, by laymen, in the midst of a busy schedule, was irrelevant to character formation (except insofar as it was divisive). This was the separatist attitude, expressing the prominence given to the idea of separation of church and state. Four school board members (Derzon, Goldman, Mrs. Hanna, and Leonard) and four principals shared this image of themselves. Along with Kaplan, the incisive Miss Cohen, the Negro Woodford, and the talkative Miss Kennedy were separatists.

Two officials did not fit neatly into these four types. The two exceptions were Miss Battistella and Coleman, the Negro school board member.

Miss Battistella was a worrier. She worried about the infiltration of Communists. She worried about the degeneracy of youth. She worried about paper work. She worried about whether everyone got his oral vaccine. She worried about violence on the streets and off it. She worried why one child wrote God "G—". She worried about labor unions, capitalism, progress, stagnation—everything under the sun, big and small, without the corollary capacity to distinguish what was of major importance and what was not. Changes in the status quo were inevitably worrisome. If a change brought about both desired and undesirable consequences, as changes usually did, she had no equipment to weigh the difference between the good and the bad.

Miss Battistella was intelligent and sensitive. She ran an extremely good elementary school, consisting largely of Jewish children. The Jews had not always been preponderant, but the school population in Miss Battistella's regime had changed. The number of Jewish families spilling over from nearby Forest Hill had increased, and they had sent their children to public school. Coincidentally, two parochial schools had recently been constructed nearby, attracting the Catholic children of the neighborhood.

Miss Battistella enjoyed serving the parents of her students, much as Farley or Rynne enjoyed it. A devoted Catholic, educated in parochial schools, she found it uncomfortable working with Jewish children. Her analogies fell flat; her spontaneous emphases were inapt; her deepest assumptions were questioned. She did not like the change in school population and would have liked to correct it by out-distancing parochial schools in the competition for Catholic talent. To win, however, she perceived she had to neutralize the religious advantage of the parochial schools by infusing the public school curriculum with increased doses of religion.

Thus, while her cognitions had more in common with those officials we have called trustees, her competitive situation made her a unionist.

We have previously described the basis of Coleman's position about religion in the public schools: the importance of introducing Negroes to a common ritual in order to assimilate them with whites. In that he emphasized the necessity of a common ritual, Coleman had a patriot self-image. It was the extensive variety of sectarian practices which he included as part of the American heritage, combined with the strength with which he insisted on superimposing this heritage upon opposed sectarian beliefs, that made his attitude more unionist than patriot.

Our array[2] is shown in Table 1.

Table 1. Self-Image of Public School Officials on Schoolhouse Religion before *Schempp*

	Unionist	*Trustee*	*Patriot*	*Separatist*	*Total*
School Board	3	0	0	4	7
Superintendents	0	0	2	0	2
Principals	7	3	5	4	19
Totals	10	3	7	8	28

Translating Self-Image into Policy Preferences

My point thus far has been that the pre-*Schempp* self-images of Midland officials in regard to religion in the schoolhouse were comfortable and deep attitudes. That a self-image fitted snugly, however, did not mean that it was explicit, thoughtout, or even conscious. Comments such as "My thinking is mixed up in my mind" or was "not firm" indicated that, at least in some cases, the self-images were below the level of ready consciousness. Generally, the individual educator had not developed his self-image into an explicitly integral position.

[2] Parenthetically, it might be noted that the more unionist the educator's self-image, the more likely was he to be a Catholic and a conservative; the more separatist was he, the more was he likely to be non-Catholic and liberal. Sex and age did not correlate at all with religious predispositions.

CATHOLIC

	UNION	TRUST	PAT.	SEP.	TOTAL
Liberal	1	0	4	1	6
Middle of Road	4	2	1	0	7
Conservative	3	1	1	0	5
	8	3	6	1	18

NON-CATHOLIC

	UNION	TRUST	PAT.	SEP.	TOTAL
Liberal	0	0	0	6	6
Middle of Road	0	0	1	1	2
Conservative	2	0	0	0	2
	2	0	1	7	10

Table 2. Self-Image of Public School Officials on Schoolhouse Religion before *Schempp* (by name)

	Unionist	*Trustee*	*Patriot*	*Separatist*	*Total*
School Board	Clancy Coleman Rizzuto			Derzon Goldman Hanna Leonard	7
Superintendents			Bartkowicz O'Hara		2
Principals	Barber Battistella Berman FitzGerald Mareno O'Brien Russo	Cagney Farley Rynne	Barrone Goldberg Mercer Murphy Toreno	Cohen Kaplan Kennedy Woodford	19

Symptomatic of the vagueness of the officials' attitudes before *Schempp* was the nearly universal apparent discrepancy between the devotional policies implied by their self-images and their actual policy preferences. Generally the officials could not convert their self-images into appropriate policies. Let me explain.

To discover what kinds of devotional practices each Midland official preferred, we asked eleven questions during the first interview. Each of the questions began, "Would you like to have this kind of religious observance in your school, or not . . . ?" Eleven different devotional practices were then described, and in response to each the individual was asked to answer that he would like the practice, dislike it, or would feel indifferent about it. Eventually, one question was dropped and two questions combined. This left nine questions which were then divided into three sets,[3] as follows:

Set 1

a. Now suppose that a teacher gives the class the opportunity to say prayers together in the classroom, any student who wished being permitted to leave the room? (Q. 1-28)

b. If a Bible-study course were given as an option and taught by a classroom teacher, how would you feel? (Q. 1-36)

[3] For further discussion, see Appendix.

c. . . . would you like an optional Bible-study course which was taught by a minister, priest, or rabbi (in classrooms within your school), depending on the individual student's choice? (Q. 1-37)

Set 2

a. How would you feel about the principal reading the Bible in morning assembly at Christmastime? (Q. 1-30)

b. What about a classroom teacher (or the principal) reading the Bible in her classroom (or at morning assembly) at the beginning of each day, all students attending? (Qq. 1-31, 32)

c. How do you feel about the student body singing hymns daily in morning assembly, all students attending? (Q. 1-34)[4]

Set 3

a. Suppose a teacher required his class to recite aloud in the classroom a prayer, all students being required to say it. Would you like or dislike such a practice . . . ? (Q. 1-27)

b. How would you feel if the principal recited a prayer at morning assembly, any student remaining silent who wished to do so? (Q. 1-29)

c. Would you like or dislike the singing of hymns at Christmastime in morning assembly, all students being in attendance? (Q. 1-33)

The situations in the first set were characterized by the isolation of the student who was not conventionally religious. In order to keep his religious citadel inviolate, he would have to identify himself as a nonparticipant and withdraw himself from group activities. In much the same way as a student who did not want to be Americanized, or taught physics, or inoculated, the student would have to bear the social stigma of being hostile to the "help" of the educational system.

The practices in the second set involved the reading or singing of materials which were sectarian and hence unfamiliar to religious persons of different sects. These exercises did not require the unconventionally religious student to absent himself from the group, how-

[4] In the Appendix I have written; "One might wonder why a preference for daily hymn singing is more Unionist than one for daily prayers. The answer rests in the largely Catholic composition of the interviewed population. To the Catholic respondents, hymns seemed to be prayers sung, hence were more sacredly charged than prayers said." For further remarks on this point and upon the cumulative modification of the Guttman scale employed in this study, see Appendix.

ever. He could close his eyes and ears to the brief exercises. Each of the practices, however, unmistakably exposed the student to the importance of religion and involved selection from obviously sectarian materials.

The exercises in the third set were the recital and singing of materials which were conventional in American society, ritualistic, brief, and frequently heard in non-religious circumstances. If any religious practices were to be thought of as part of the patriotic heritage, these common carols and routinized prayers were they.

These sets corresponded to three of our four self-images. A unionist, wishing to deflect a child's religious development into proper channels, would presumably feel obliged to use social pressure to obtain a child's participation in various religious programs sponsored by the school (Set 1, or the stigma policy). Likewise, a trustee predictably would like to introduce a non-coercive, but variegated, sectarianism into his school (Set 2, or the exposure policy). Third, we would anticipate that a patriot would be satisfied with a unison recital of a well-known prayer or Christmas carols (Set 3, or the commonplace policy). Finally, an educator who was a separatist in his feelings and intellect would reject all three sets of observances (the elimination policy).

The interviews were scored as follows. If the official responded positively to at least two of the practices in any one set, he scored a plus on that set; otherwise he received a minus. It was anticipated that it would become increasingly easier to score positively on each successive set. That is, if a person had a plus with respect to the coercive practices of Set 1, the prediction was that he would score plusses on the voluntarist practices described in Sets 2 and 3 as well. This expectation, which proved correct under the circumstances, was comparable to predicting that a person who behaved like a unionist wanted all the devotional practices desired by trustee and patriot officials and a little more.

A person scoring a plus on all three sets was put in Group I (the stigma policy, supposedly equivalent to the unionist self-image). At the other end of the scale were those who scored minuses on all three sets; these advocates of the elimination policy were put in Group IV and were the counterparts of those who were separatists. Between were Group II (scoring a minus on Set 1 but pluses on the exposure and commonplace sets), corresponding to the trustee's preferences, and Group III (scoring a plus on Set 3 only), representing the commonplace policies implied by the patriot attitude.

Table 3. Scoring the Policy Preferences

Set	*1*	*2*	*3*
Group			
I Stigma	+	+	+
II Exposure	—	+	+
III Commonplace	—	—	+
IV Elimination	—	—	—

When I compared the results described by the policy preference index and my earlier attitudinal analysis, the results were as follows.

Table 4. Equivocation between Self-Image and Policy Preference before *Schempp*

Policy Preference / Attitude	*I* (Stigma)	*II* (Exposure)	*III* (Commonplace)	*IV* (Elimination)	Total
Unionist	1	4	4	1	10
Trustee	0	1	2	0	3
Patriot	3	1	1	2	7
Separatist	0	0	0	8	8
	4	6	7	11	28

Underlined numbers represent persons with "unequivocal" attitudes.

Table 4 shows a high degree of equivocation between self-images and policies, as I conceived equivocation. By my definition, seventeen of the twenty-eight officials actually would have promulgated policies at variance with the implications of their self-image. I say that these seventeen officials were "equivocal" because they harbored two distinctly different and contradictory ideas—one of philosophy and one of policy—about a single subject matter, with no present ability to resolve the incompatability.

To bring the details of the table out more clearly: of the twenty officials who held non-separatist attitudes, only three—Coleman, Farley, and Mrs. Toreno—would have instituted devotional policies in their schools consistent with their self-images. When Rizzuto, a unionist, urged an elimination policy (Group IV), the equivocation (as I have defined it) was remarkable. Four officials—Miss Barrone, Miss Mercer, Murphy, and Dr. Bartkowicz—wanted more religion

Table 5. Equivocation between Self-Image and Policy Preference before *Schempp* (by name)

PREFERENCE ATTITUDE	GROUP I (*Stigma*)	GROUP II (*Exposure*)	GROUP III (*Commonplace*)	GROUP IV (*Elimination*)
Unionist	Coleman	Berman FitzGerald Mareno Russo	Barber Battistella Clancy O'Brien	Rizzuto
Trustee	(None)	Farley	Cagney Rynne	(None)
Patriot	Barrone Mercer Murphy	Bartkowicz	Toreno	O'Hara Goldberg
Separatist	(None)	(None)	(None)	Derzon Goldman Hanna Leonard Cohen Kaplan Kennedy Woodford

than their self-images implied. On the other hand, thirteen officials originally wanted less religious practices than their feelings and cognitions consistently supported. Why this highly inconsistent state of affairs?

Equivocation and Social Commitment

We are all capable of harboring inconsistent attitudes, and Midland officials were no exception to the human rule. To take one example (which could be multiplied manifold), the alert Russo said, "Nowadays . . . kids develop with no sense of morals"; three questions later, in describing the reaction of his predominantly lower class pupils to the new and "beautiful" school building, he said: "Why, look at these white walls—spotless. The only ones who misbehave are the adults. Why, those kids running hell bent will turn the corner to avoid going on the grass." Russo would have seemed a fool if he had uttered those two remarks in a debating society, but in Russo's environment nobody made an issue of this inconsistency. He was never motivated to smooth out his thoughts.

Similarly, in the matter of schoolhouse religion, most principals until the time of the first interview had not had an issue made of their attitudes on school prayers. Their social environment was typically as harmonious as that of Miss O'Brien's. Few had previously suffered as Miss Kennedy had. Let us look at these two elderly Irish, spinster, elementary school principals: Miss O'Brien with her highly equivocal attitude, Miss Kennedy with her atypically consistent demands.

Molly O'Brien was still an active principal because her personnel records gave her an age three years younger than her real years. She was devoted to teaching young children, especially the underprivileged, the retarded, and the deprived. Her nineteenth-century school was buried in the midst of the most neglected slum in the city.

She was a conversational experience, for she was a Catholic ideologist. If one gave her the most secular-sounding question, within two sentences she would bring in such incidental, but not illogically related, data as: "I have just learned that George Washington fasted on Sundays"; discuss the excommunication of the "brilliant" Father Feeney; or give a critique of the editorial policy of the diocesan newspaper. In describing her graduate work, she picked out of her memory an English course she took at Midland University and began discussing a paper she wrote for it: *Shakespeare Was a Catholic*. She was an unabashed religious missionary among her pupils. The attitude structure in which her Catholicism was central was what Lane would describe as "high-density, closely articulated,"[5] with logical connections forged between her religion and a vast number of ideas. To provide one homely illustration, Miss O'Brien ardently supported Negro civil rights.

God does not place brains in one race. I say to my children, Do you read the Bible? How many people did God make? Just two. We are all descendants from God. They [the first Negroes] are really your great-great-great grandfathers. God gave us all these relatives!"

Yet despite the logical coherence of the ideas stemming from her Catholicism, she did not advocate the stigma policy we might have predicted would have been consistent with her unionist self-image. She placed in Group III, preferring the commonplace policy.

If we assume that she had not made a logically proper linkage between her self-image and her preferences for practice, we confront the question: why not?

[5] Robert E. Lane, *Political Ideology* (New York: Free Press of Glencoe, 1962), p. 464.

Her environment had never pushed her to be consistent, had never made her take issue with the status quo in schoolhouse religion as she had found it. In her school she had two or three Jewish children, a number of Negro Protestants, and some Jehovah's Witnesses; the preponderant majority was Catholic. On schoolhouse religion, the lower-class parents of her children, typically working couples, deferred to her judgment. On this issue the P.T.A. was never inquisitive or obstreperous.

Miss O'Brien did not have completely smooth sailing on all matters: there were invariable complaints about poor discipline and poor achievement, but no one ever brought up schoolhouse religion for Miss O'Brien to think about.

Contrast Miss Kennedy, whose school was set in the middle of one of the old Jewish sections in the city; some of her staff were Jewish; and her school population was Jewish, Negro, and Catholic, in diminishing proportions. She recognized the importance to children of "saying prayers in early childhood"; yet without equivocation, her mind had been made up on the issue of a daily prayer before the Supreme Court decision. "My philosophy is that there is no place for it in public schools." She had transformed her attitude into the logically consistent policy. Why this clarity of views?

One clue derived from my first impression of Miss Kennedy's school. As I walked into the building at lunchtime one weekday, three or four well-dressed mothers were converging on Miss Kennedy's tiny office. The P.T.A. of the school, presently presided over by a Jewish woman of considerable ability, was, and had always been, extremely active. The relationship between it and Miss Kennedy was far from harmonious, for its members were candid, critical, intensely interested in the children, organized and sufficiently well-to-do to have time to badger Miss Kennedy, any time of the day. Miss Kennedy had a monkey on her back, and her critics were more than sullen—they were mutinous.

She had been principal of this school since 1933.

When I was first appointed to this school, there were quite a lot of Jewish children . . . One teacher, a Protestant, a little country girl from Canton, Ohio, read the Nativity. But she didn't stop there. She went on to the Crucifixion and said, "The Jews killed Christ." One boy, Bob Newman (now a lawyer, back here in Midland) said that was not so. The teacher said, "We'll talk about this at Easter." A few weeks later Mrs. Newman came to see me. She said she would have reported me to the superintendent, but her attorney had looked me up in the files and found that I had never said anything anti-Semitic. (Did you hear what I said about those files? Why, that's tactics like the Fascists used.) I said that I did not know about it, that it had no place in the public schools. I went to the teacher to put a stop to it. She said she would not stop it. I told her to get out. No one has a right to hurt a child.

She described in quick order five more incidents in which parents or the P.T.A. had criticized her and forced her to eliminate school devotional practices involving crèches, Christmas carols, readings from the Protestant Bible, the production of a Nativity play, and the presentation of a Hannukkah pantomime.

These six incidents, related in less than fifteen minutes time, were later supplemented with further accounts of P.T.A. difficulties in the area of religious practices. Clearly, Miss Kennedy's attitudes on schoolhouse religion had been made an issue by an aggressive P.T.A. Until she got some kind of coincidence between her thoughts, feelings, and policies in school, she undoubtedly attracted complaints from every corner of the neighborhood. When she decided that her community would continue to be a bane until she resolved her inconsistency, she accommodated the community. She could not afford to be equivocal; she had to make up her mind on the place of prayers in her public school long before the Supreme Court did on prayers in public schools generally.

The inference to be gained from the high degree of discrepancy between self-image and policy preferences which we found in most of the officials' attitudes is that, except in a few neighborhoods, the matter of school prayers had never before been an issue. The administrators were never coerced into committing themselves to transforming their thoughts into an unequivocal statement of policy. The two or three Jewish families who sent their children to Miss O'Brien's school certainly never objected, never caused Miss O'Brien trouble, never asked Why. In budgeting her time, she would have been irrational to worry over an academic matter. The intellectual frustrations of her underprivileged students gave her enough of consequence to mull upon.

The mandatory language of the *Schempp* decision—the law—changed that dormant state of affairs in Midland schools. It elevated schoolhouse religion to the status of an issue. What is the nature of law? And, before *Schempp* how did the officials feel about lawmakers, especially the lawmaker which was to make an issue of their attitudes about schoolhouse religion—the Supreme Court of the United States?

V

Original Attitudes toward the Law and the Supreme Court

Schempp was interpreted by the Midland school board as compelling local agencies such as itself to promulgate a policy in public schools forbidding "prayers or other devotional exercises on school premises." In terms of the policy preferences which I have just described, the Court's preference (if we can call an order a preference) would be eliminationist. Its rule was out of line with the preferred policies of seventeen officials, the four who urged the stigma policy (Group I), the six who urged the exposure policy (Group II), and the seven who favored a commonplace policy (Group III).

Equally important as the rule was the ethical rationalization of the rule contained in the majority opinion. The attitude the majority opinion prescribed and the empirical propositions explicit in its argument amounted to what I have called the separatist self-image. Its most elevated expression appeared in the final paragraph of the opinion which Justice Tom Clark wrote for the Court.

> The place of religion in our society is an exalted one, achieved through a long tradition of reliance on the home, the church and the inviolable citadel of the individual heart and mind. We have come to recognize through bitter experience that it is not within the power of government to invade that citadel, whether its purpose or effect be to aid or oppose.[1]

The Court's opinion did more than express the separatist self-image. It also set forth the opposing attitudes and did its best to knock each down with reason and logic. For example, it gave words to the patriot's

[1] 374 U. S., at 226.

position: that certain conventional prayers are appropriate so long as they are intended by the educators not to promote religious belief but to bring about "the promotion of moral values, the contradiction to the materialistic trends of our times, the perpetuation of our institutions and the teaching of literature."[2]

The Court's rejoinder was that the educator's intent was not a sufficient basis for classifying a religiously derived exercise as secular; just as important was the effect of the exercise upon the student. If in fact its primary effect was on the religious beliefs of some students, then, irrespective of what the teacher intended to accomplish, an exercise no longer was secular.

The opinion also voiced the misgivings of people who held a trustee self-image ("Unless these religious exercises are permitted a 'religion of secularism' is established in the schools"[3]). The Court's response was to point to the limited scope of the public school and its traditional interdependence on other American institutions; public schools are organized "on the premise that secular education can be isolated from all religious teaching so that the school can inculcate all needed temporal knowledge and . . . after the individual has been instructed in worldly wisdom he will be better fitted to choose his religion."[4]

Finally, while the opinion did not make explicit the unionist self-image, its rebuttal was the axiom from which the opinion departed: "The government is neutral, and, while protecting all [religious opinions], it prefers none, and it disparages none"[5]—not even agnosticism, insidious though it might seem to some teachers.

The Court's opinion was thus at odds with all three non-separatist self-images variously held by twenty of the twenty-eight officials in the Midland school system. Furthermore, it may even have been inconsistent with the thinking of some of the eight separatists. Before *Schempp,* at least Goldman, Miss Kennedy, and Leonard had argued for the elimination of all religious discussion in the schools, even in comparative religion courses. The Court, on the other hand, spoke favorably of comparative religion courses in a public school curriculum, including a study of the Bible for "its literary and historic qualities . . . when presented objectively as part of a secular program of educa-

[2] 374 U. S., at 223.
[3] 374 U. S. at 225.
[4] 374 U. S., at 218.
[5] 374 U. S., at 215.

tion."[6] Thus, in all, twenty-three of twenty-eight officials found in *Schempp* ideas which conflicted with their original attitudes.

Attitudes toward the Supreme Court, Courts, and Law

The backlash hypothesis, you will recall, anticipates that in a clash between the legal command of *Schempp* and the non-separatist attitudes of Midland educators, the educators might attempt to derogate the Supreme Court as a first step in justifying non-compliance with it. If in their minds the Supreme Court's reputation were already sullied, if its prestige were so little connected to consequential attitudes, deprecation of it and ultimate non-compliance would be an easy way of resolving the conflict between their beliefs and the law. If, on the other hand, the Court had a positive reputation and were associated with important personal experiences, negative treatment of the Court would be difficult if not impossible. For this reason the Court's position in the officials' mental frames of reference was of great importance, and I tried to discover it.

Two preliminary remarks on method are necessary. First, as I searched for clues to attitudes about the Supreme Court, I found that its reputation was intertwined with the prestige of judges and lawyers in general. The American Supreme Court was regarded as the zenith of all legal institutions. More exactly, when a respondent was questioned about the Supreme Court of the United States and incidentally recalled a pleasant or distressful memory of a lesser judge or lawyer, it invariably happened that his feelings about the Supreme Court turned out to be congruent with his attraction or hostility to the legal person he mentioned. The interviews indicated good reason to believe that any official who displayed animosity to judges or lawyers was in fact predisposed unfavorably toward the Supreme Court. Conversely, favorable remarks about judges or lawyers indicated a liking for the Court.

Second, the method of determining the favorable or hostile character of the respondents' attitudes to the Supreme Court consisted of finding their earliest recollection of law-related events and determining whether it was a pleasant or distressful memory. The theory behind this method was not that these oldest memories caused the favorable or hostile character of the attitude but that they indicated it. The as-

[6] 374 U. S., at 225.

sumption was that the impulse to remember an old incident about law was rooted in the individual's feelings about law. Aggrieved, an individual would remember grievances; satisfied, he would indicate that satisfaction by recalling satisfactory events. In short, I believed that a person was more likely to recall incidents consonant with his feelings than events at odds with them.[7]

At this juncture the reader should take note of these ersatz methods of determining the respondents' feelings toward the lawmaker. These methods were developed after the interviews were completed, and the results of their application to the content of the interviews coincided with my intuition about the respondents, an intuition which was tutored equally by their words and by their gestures, facial expressions, and hesitancies, by nonverbal cues that become invisible on the typewritten record. As I have said in the Methodological Postscript, no interjudge reliability tests were used to check my bias of interpretation. In subsequent studies of this kind, scholars will need more definitive and objective methods of measuring this concept of feelings toward the lawmaker.

With this caveat in mind, we are in a position to examine the results. I identified the attitudes of all the respondents but three—Miss Kennedy, Miss Battistella, and Mrs. Toreno. Of the remaining twenty-five, eleven[8] had positive responses to the Supreme Court, courts, and lawyers. "Prestige," writes Neustadt, "counts in power by establishing some checks upon resistance from the men engaged in governing."[9] With these eleven officials engaged in governing in Midland, the American Supreme Court had some prestige. Hence, were they to have developed a dislike for the Court because of their distaste for *Schempp,* they would have had to square their hostility with their predisposition to admire the justices.

[7] Further discussion of method appears in the Appendix.

[8] Barrone, Coleman, Derzon, Goldberg, Goldman, Hanna, Leonard, Mercer, Murphy, Rynne, and Woodford. For example, Woodford told this story: "We used to rent from a railroad man. He used to tell me I'd be president of the United States. Later on I went to live with this man. We used to hold moot trials. We got a kick out of it. It was a lot of fun. He'd be the prosecutor, witness, defendant, or judge. He was quite a knowledgeable man, a frustrated lawyer. Twelve of us boarded with him, and every Thursday night we did this."

[9] Richard Neustadt, *Presidential Power* (New York: John Wiley & Sons, 1960), p. 90.

Fourteen officials,[10] however, had quite the opposite attitude toward legal institutions. For example, Mareno, the senior high school principal, when asked for his childhood memory of law courts, recalled that he "once visited the city court a long time ago. All the stew bums were lined up, and I didn't stay long." Miss O'Brien, recalling her childhood, remembered the children of the lawyer next door writing, "Go to hell, Irish Catholics: go home." "You know where those children got that idea?" she asked. "That judge had one policy for home and one for the court." Hypocrisy, pretentiousness, latent unfairness—if judges had such vices, their derogation was hardly a cause for tears.

Among this hostile majority of officials was Dr. Clancy. He was a friendly bear of a man, a pediatrician sufficiently skillful in his profession to conduct seminars for graduate pediatricians at Midland University. Furthermore, thanks to his wife, the daughter of a politically powerful contractor, Dr. Clancy knew practically everyone, high and middle, newly rich and on the make. His acceptance of a position on the school board, his first governmental office, had turned his professional life upside down. He had had to give up medical teaching because of political demands on his time. The political realm, however, was not easy for him, because he was not so good with words. He was neither felicitous nor facile, especially burdened as he was with a strange, new political vocabulary, so unrelated to medical terms.

To Clancy, law was part of the political realm. How did he think of it? Law was cold, unresponsive to life and to the people. Even though a school board member was a lawmaker, Clancy shunned the thought that he had any connection with lawmakers, with persons engaged in politics. During the interview he reiterated a number of times the distinction, "I'm not speaking as a politician, but just as a plain ordinary citizen." Politics, the process of lawmaking, amounted to nothing more than temporizing with crackpots, quibbling over infuriating distinctions, and engaging in endless argument washed (as Holmes put it) "with cynical acid."[11] It was all alien and distasteful. What was more, "it's dangerous." The Supreme Court, equally "hard

[10] Barber, Bartkowicz, Berman, Cagney, Clancy, Cohen, Farley, FitzGerald, Kaplan, Mareno, O'Brien, O'Hara, Rizzuto, and Russo.

[11] Oliver Wendell Holmes, Jr., "The Path of the Law" (address delivered January 8, 1897), reprinted in *The World of Law* (ed., Ephraim London) Vol. II (New York: Simon and Schuster, 1960), p. 618.

and cold," aloof from "the people," with its "calculated manner," personified the law for Clancy. It was the suspicion that the justices were in fact "set apart from the concerns of the community"[12] which made the Supreme Court so objectionable to him.

The Sources of the Feelings

Why was it true for such a large proportion of Midland educators that the Court, courts, and lawyers rated so poorly? Clancy provided an answer worth remarking. He told this story part way through the second interview.

> I got pinched going thirty miles per hour in a twenty-five-mile-an-hour zone. The policeman said I was clocked on radar. Now, I don't believe in radar. But that's it. They got a law, and we have to obey it. It cost me thirty dollars—but I had to go along with him.

From Clancy's vantage point, the law was nothing more than policemen and radar. The law prevented people from doing what they wanted to do. It deprived them of freedom, frustrated their rights, and told them they were doing wrong. No one likes to be told he is doing wrong.

The hallmark of the law for the majority of Midland officials before the prayer decision was its preventive aspect, even for such sophisticated political men as Chairman Rizzuto and Superintendent Bartkowicz. Both these men, at the very time when they thought they were praising the Supreme Court, perceived it as an inhibitor. "It's healthy to have the Court step in to say, 'Wait a minute' " (Rizzuto). "I think of the Supreme Court as a reaction . . . It keeps things on an even keel" (Bartkowicz).

The view of law as an inhibitor has its parallels in childhood. The youngster confronts laws which he does not understand and which frustrate his desires to explore the world in his fashion. His parents, the crosswalk guards, the teachers, even his own contemporaries tell him he is wrong when he violates the law. In the majority of cases he comes to dislike the law and his subordination to it. Then this resentment slips into adulthood; a vague feeling of indignity attaches to legal compliance. Miss O'Brien, the devout Irish lady, said at the close of the

[12] Felix Frankfurter, *Law and Politics* (New York: Harcourt, Brace, 1939), p. 108. "It would seem that multitudes of Americans seriously believe that the nine Justices . . . are set apart from the concerns of the community . . ."

second interview, "We would not need civil rights if we forgave them as we would have them forgive us." Perhaps she really wished its converse: "If we had no civil rights, we could forgive them as we would have them forgive us." Law, in short, is demeaning.

Not all Midland officials felt this way about the legal system. In contrast let us look at Woodford's views, as he expressed them in the two interviews. Woodford was a capacious man, gentle and reflective. He had been in the school system for thirteen years, as a teacher, a director of community relations in a populous Negro neighborhood, and finally principal of a school in the better Negro area. He was Episcopalian, liberal, a native of Midland, and a Negro.

Woodford observed that the legal system was a liberating force in his life. From what did the law liberate? In the first place, it freed people from endless disputes. The Supreme Court was like an umpire in a baseball game, letting the teams get on with the contest by ending bickering.

Second, it freed men from the oppression of the marketplace. It allowed homes to be redeemed after the mortgage had been foreclosed. It opened up private employment opportunities. It provided in the public sector the training and discipline which the marketplace had monopolized for the white man, the very skills and discipline which were indispensable if a man was to be made independent and able to assert himself. Woodford, quite stirred, remarked: "I'm interested in it [the Constitution] because I feel my own sustenance is in it. Here, if I can't depend on it, I'm in trouble."

Dahl[13] has made the point that Negroes have had little choice but to turn to the public sector because of their exclusion from private economic endeavor. With no opportunities available in the free enterprise system, upward-bound Negroes have looked to the government as something warm and receptive. In attending to the ways of government, they have incidentally come to see the utility of law, courts, and legislatures. Woodford stopped talking in the middle of the second interview, walked across the room, and without the slightest uncertainty dug out a copy of the United States Constitution from the bookcase. When he finished talking about it and closed the book, he summed up: "As I see it, the important thing is the enhancement of the Court" —the Supreme Court of the United States was the Constitution personified.

13 Robert A. Dahl, *Who Governs?* (New Haven: Yale University Press, 1961), p. 294.

In the third place, the legal process unchained people from the constraints of local public opinion. Woodford talked about the importance of the state reapportionment decisions to Negroes, recognizing the important link between the elimination of rural over-representation and increasing Negro influence in the legislative process. Up to now pretty powerful interests had used the legal process to inculcate bigotry and were still doing so in the state legislatures in the South (e.g., Jim Crow laws). Woodford recognized that reapportionment would transfer control of lawmaking to new hands, making it possible to teach people to forget skin color. It took him a long time to see the liberating effect of law, because it had so long been used to oppress him. But clearly legal institutions could and did educate public opinion. For good or ill, widespread social learning resulted from legislation, blunting and even reversing established patterns of social conformity, releasing people from the constraints of their neighbors. "It's very exciting," concluded Woodford.

There was, in the fourth place, another effect. While I talked with Woodford, a grateful mother barged into his office to thank him for a favor done her child and to give him a present. He refused the gift, invoking a school board regulation prohibiting its acceptance. He was able to get on with his job of administering the school without being put in the woman's debt, yet he kept his refusal cordial and impersonal. The law, while nominally forbidding him from taking gifts, actually gave him privacy within his job and protection from outside obligations.

Thus, the law freed Woodford and others like him from four snares: indecision, market forces, social pressures, and unwanted intrusions. Let me digress from our narrative. On July 10, 1963 the Senate Commerce Committee took testimony from Secretary of State Dean Rusk, on the then proposed Civil Rights Act of 1964. The following interchange took place between Rusk and Strom Thurmond, Senator from South Carolina.

SENATOR THURMOND: Mr. Secretary, there are many who sincerely view proposals for the National Government to force private property owners to extend services on their property to persons against their will as a deprivation of their property rights, without due process of law. Do you believe that the problems which you have presented here today justify a legislative act which at the very least diminishes freedom in the use of property which each property owner now has?

MR. RUSK: Well, I could not agree, sir, that such a law would diminish freedom. The purpose of law in a free society is to enlarge freedom by letting each know what kind of conduct to expect from the other. And it is through our laws that personal freedom is not only protected, but constantly enlarged, so we can pursue our orbit with a minimum of collisions.[14]

The interchange summed up the double aspect of law: the inhibiting and the liberating. The fourteen Midland officials who disliked the Supreme Court, courts, and lawyers shared a viewpoint like Thurmond's—law was coercive, deprivational, constraining. The eleven officials who positively valued the Supreme Court and the legal process inclined to the Rusk vision of law as an instrument of freedom, permitting individuals to "pursue our orbit with a minimum of collisions." By synchronizing social expectations and thereby reducing the risk of human collision, legal messages enabled men to achieve a measure of dignity.

The Vagueness of These Feelings

Russo, the thirty-five-year-old principal, originally had a negative predisposition toward the Supreme Court. It was clear in his first interview that he believed that persons who saw things differently than he did were wrong. Parents were myopic; the press was poor; fellow teachers were fusty; businessmen were dishonest; and people did not have guts.

Russo hated to be told he was wrong by people in authority, and he treated the Supreme Court with no more respect than he did all the other "hypocrites in high places." Russo voiced an argument, current a generation ago when Roosevelt was attempting to pack the Supreme Court in 1937. Nonetheless, it served Russo as a suitable vehicle for expressing his hostility toward the justices. ("I don't particularly care for allowing the Supreme Court justices to stay for life; there is a decline of mental powers and one old justice might cast a deciding vote in a crucial case.")

Russo talked distrustfully in the first interview, expressing resentment against the system, venting a general animosity which spilled over up to the Court. His hostility, however, was without much force. He had previously made no important decisions on the basis of this diffused negative attitude. There were no neighboring opinions inter-

[14] U. S. Senate, Committee on Commerce, 88th Congress, 1st Sess., Hearing's on S.1732, A Bill to eliminate discrimination in Public Accommodations affecting Interstate Commerce, Part I, p. 315.

related with his reaction to the Court. His feelings were footloose and irrelevant, a receptacle for hostilities with other origins. His attitude about the Court was a piece of filler material, to be invoked when persons came seeking answers, which he did not really have, to questions he thought he should be up on.

When Russo was questioned again a year later, after the Court's prayer decision, he described the impotence of these original ideas.

> Whether my regard or interest in the Supreme Court has increased? Both my interest and regard have increased. Before, I was very complacent. They were, in my thinking, involved in the economic realm—trust busting and all that. But these things were not an issue with me, like civil rights is. Now you look at every issue, and some aspect of civil rights is there. As to my regard for it, I never had any before. I was hardly conscious of it, kind of like having a mother and father, and it never occurs to you whether you do or you don't love them.

What did Russo mean when he said the Supreme Court had never before been involved in anything that had been an "issue with me"? Conversely, what happened to a person's thinking when the Court did become an issue?

I separated the officials into two classes based on definiteness of the reaction they had to the Court. One class responded relatively spontaneously, intensely, supported by information readily recalled. The other class reacted self-consciously, without passion, their efforts to remember events related to the Court markedly labored. The definite kind of reaction was invariably unequivocal—that is, if a person reacted spontaneously, his remarks about the Court, courts, and lawyers tended all to be of one character, either purely favorable or purely negative. The detached, emotionless, labored reaction, on the other hand, was more likely to be equivocal; in one sentence a person would offer a positive remark, but in the next he would level a harsh criticism.

The more I compared those officials who spoke definitely with those who spoke less decisively, the clearer it became that the Court was of far greater importance to the definite officials. In their political frames of reference, the judiciary, as Lane put it, was "bolted down,"[15] which was not the case with their vaguer brethren. The commitment of those who reacted with passion to or against the court prohibited any concessions to the opposite judgment. With those who spoke vaguely it seemed that the latest information about the Court actually affected

[15] Robert E. Lane, *Political Ideology* (New York: Free Press of Glencoe, 1962), p. 464.

their feelings toward it. In distinguishing judgmental from dissonance theory, Cohen and Brehm put their fingers on the distinction I noticed among the officials.

> When we speak of "judgmental processes" . . . we refer to the notion of information processing . . . any incoming bit of information is given its due, and the individual makes some compromise judgment between the information and his existing cognitions . . . The analogy here is to some estimate he makes of all the various cognitions, to some arithmetic average of his cognitions.
>
> On the other hand, an unequivocal dissonance process exists . . . when there is some commitment to a given position. Once this occurs, the person cannot process information and make some compromise judgment; he must accommodate his cognitions to his commitment. In effect, one pole of the inconsistency is now fixed . . .
>
> The point here is that dissonance processes have the flavor of an either-or phenomenon; judgmental processes, on the other hand, admit of a compromise all along the information continuum. Dissonance implies a distortion or discontinuity due to commitment . . . The judgmental process . . . implies a more "rational" assessment of different pieces of inconsistent information in terms of existing cognitions, and a resultant compromise solution.[16]

To adapt the point, for some officials the Supreme Court fitted into a "judgmental process." Their vague attitude about the Supreme Court admitted of compromise. "Any inconsistent bit of information" was likely to be thrown into the equation, and the attitude was subject to continual adjustment by the addition of further factors. On the other hand, some officials placed the Court in a "dissonance process." They were definite and unequivocal about the Court; a degree of commitment to or against the Court had already occurred. Such a dissonance process refused equal access to all information—it discriminated. There was a skewing, a bias, a calculated sifting inherent in an unequivocal attitude. Adverse information, far from altering a judgment about the Supreme Court, was itself altered to fit the individual's prevailing feelings; otherwise, it was rejected and forgotten altogether. Magnetism, not a mathematical average, was the image appropriate to some of the officials' feelings about the Court; the existing predisposition attracted only congenial information about the Court and left the residue uncollected.

A definite attitude about the Supreme Court seemed to attract a lot of information, but of one kind; I found I could separate those officials

[16] *Brehm and Cohen,* pp. 105-6.

who had a lot of one-sided information from the other officials who did not. Of those educators who spoke of the Court, courts, or lawyers frequently and with sentiments of only one kind, I said they had definite attitudes. On the other hand, there were officials who seemed to have little information about the Court or only a mixed bag of it; their vague and equivocal thinking resembled a judgmental rather than a dissonance process. The interviews with Russo, for example, contained frequent equivocations. In the original interview, he disparaged the Court because of the declining mental powers of its members, and in the same breath asserted, "This country is as strong as it is because of the Court."

Before the prayer ban, for whom was the Court a matter of commitment? Who of the twenty-eight officials had definite attitudes? Excluding Goldman, nine were definite; five (Miss Barrone, Coleman, Professor Hanna, Leonard, and Woodford) were definitely favorable; and four (Berman, Mareno, Miss O'Brien and Miss O'Hara) were definitely hostile.[17]

What had caused the Court to become a definite commitment in their thinking? The best that I can say is that somehow some particular decision had intervened in the past into some important areas of consciousness of these nine committed individuals. Woodford and Coleman, both Negroes, were brought in touch with the Court by the 1954 desegregation decision. Leonard's early experience of "teaching colonies of Jehovah's Witnesses" in a Midwestern town coincided with the *Barnette* decision (exempting Witness children from the pledging of allegiance). Miss Barrone's attitudes about the Court seem to have crystallized about her direct experience with the *Barnette* and *McCollum* decisions.

When I tried to see why the four officials with definitely negative attitudes held the views they did, the clues became extremely elusive. Miss O'Hara had been principal in a Jewish neighborhood school in 1948, and her feeling was that the *McCollum* case had divided the community, exacerbated deep feelings, and shattered a spirit of compromise. For Berman, Mareno, and Miss O'Brien, it seemed that Senator Joseph McCarthy's attack on the Supreme Court had crystallized their attitudes. In Miss O'Brien especially, who applauded the results of the desegregation decision, wholehearted hostility toward the Court was not easy. But McCarthy had drawn the issue as Communism versus Americanism, and the Court, as McCarthy had pointed out, frequently erred on this issue. Soft-spoken and smiling all the

[17] For further discussion, see Appendix.

while, Miss O'Brien recalled that "There were three [Justices] who upheld a Communist in invoking the Fifth Amendment." For these four officials, but only for these four, it was impossible to concede some virtue to the Supreme Court of the United States.

The twenty-eight officials may be classed (Table 6) according to their original predispositions toward the Supreme Court, courts, and lawyers.

Table 6. Attitudes toward Supreme Court, Courts, and Lawyers before *Schempp*

Positive		Indeterminate	Negative	
Definitely (6)	*Vaguely* (5)	(3)	*Vaguely* (10)	*Definitely* (4)
Barrone	Derzon	Battistella	Barber	Berman
Coleman	Goldberg	Kennedy	Bartkowicz	Mareno
Goldman	Mercer	Toreno	Cagney	O'Brien
Hanna	Murphy		Clancy	O'Hara
Leonard	Rynne		Cohen	
Woodford			Farley	
			FitzGerald	
			Kaplan	
			Rizzuto	
			Russo	

On the slim basis of our data, I can make a stab at describing an American pattern of adjustment to legal institutions. At some point before reaching maturity, most individuals develop some vague frustration with people who lay down the law. The individual develops a negative response to such people—"a fear of the law," as Clancy put it. Ordinarily in a free country such as the United States this repulsion from the law is not strong; it is not related to attitudes of importance.

As the individual matures and exposes himself to wider experience, he gathers information. Since his initial reaction to the law was mild, his inchoate negative feelings do not repel positive cognitions about the law. Rather, information is attracted helter-skelter and processed in a kind of ambiguity.

This pattern of an underlying hostility to the law that is tempered by positive remembrances would describe a large number of Midland officialdom just before *Schempp* became the law of the land. Inconsistent cognitions existed side by side comfortably and within a threshold of tolerance. No sleep was lost over the vague disorder of their thoughts.

What would happen when the prayer cases would make the Court an issue in the consciousness of these officials? On the basis of the experience of those nine officials with definite attitudes, I would predict that when the Court touched these heretofore rather vague officials, they would be forced to make some kind of decision or commitment. They would have to come to grips with their compromise judgments, and there would be a tendency for them to search their memories of law-related events, selectively discarding discrepant reminiscences and thereafter looking only for that information about the justices which would bolster their commitment to or against the Supreme Court—that is, experience would lead them to substitute a dissonance process for a previous judgmental process.

The pattern points up the importance of the circumstances existing when the Court first forces commitment by the individual. Inconsistent feelings, theretofore impotent, tend to get fixed into a wider organization of attitudes. Alteration of them thereafter is much more difficult and delicate a task.

Robert McCloskey has suggested that the Supreme Court has two kinds of supporters—"those who venerate it" and "those who happen to be gratified by the course of policy the judges are pursuing at the moment."[18] Such may be part of the case, but he has omitted a crucial group of supporters—those who at some time or another have had to commit themselves to support the Court in a situation where equivocation was impossible. Once touched by the Court, such persons have stable commitments about the Court.

Courts and Schoolhouse Religion

The description of the original predispositions of Midland educators toward religion and the Supreme Court is now complete. Of the eleven officials favorably disposed to the Court, courts, and lawyers, it is worth remarking that six held non-separatist attitudes about schoolhouse religion. Among the fourteen officials negatively disposed to the Court, only two were separatists. I now turn to describing the impact of the Supreme Court on, and the issue it raised in, the personal lives of each of these twenty-eight men and women.

[18] Robert G. McCloskey, *The American Supreme Court* (Chicago: University of Chicago Press, 1960), p. 72.

VI

The Clash between Law and Attitudes

What did each of the twenty-eight officials do in the face of his disagreement (or agreement in eight instances) with the United States Supreme Court decision in *Schempp?* Why did his reaction take the particular form it did? And why did it not take other forms? These questions are at the heart of my inquiry, and it is time now to begin to grapple with them.

I start this chapter by numerically arraying the results of the clash between the law of Schempp and the attitudes of the officials. Then, using dissonance theory to provide perspective on the events, I will describe what I believe were the human dynamics which underlay these numbers.[1]

The Numerical Results

In Chapter IV I distinguished four self-images relating to religion in the Midland public schools: unionist, trustee, patriot, and separatist. These four types were assumed to be on a continuum, with the unionist and the separatist at the extremes, representing the more ardent demands for the inclusion and exclusion of schoolhouse religion. As a

[1] As the reader will see, this chapter is an admixture of quantification, theory, and surmise. Relatively crude numerical tools have helped to classify; then theory has been employed to raise fruitful questions; and, finally, surmise has been applied to give tentative answers. Someday soon a new study—a better study—will come to test the surmise, corroborating some, disputing the rest, asking more probing questions, which require more sophisticated surmise, and so on and so forth. Thus, the process of social science will continue, scratching the surface, guessing the way to the truth, seeing the light, only to find deeper surfaces to scratch, more complicated routes to truth to imagine, and more, now undreamed of, patterns to detect.

result of the two interviews, I could characterize each of the twenty-eight Midland respondents in terms of the type of self-image before and after the Supreme Court's decision. The table below reveals the changes made by the respondents.

Table 7. Self-Image of Public School Officials on Schoolhouse Religion before and after *Schempp*

	AFTER:				
BEFORE	*Union*	*Trust*	*Patriot*	*Separ*	*Total*
Union	7	0	1	2	10
Trust	1	0	2	0	3
Patriot	0	0	4	3	7
Separ	0	0	1	7	8
Total	8	0	8	12	28

Non-changers underlined

Table 8. Self-Image of Public School Officials on Schoolhouse Religion before and after *Schempp* (by name)

	AFTER:			
BEFORE	*Union*	*Trust*	*Patriot*	*Separ*
Union	Barber Battistella Berman Clancy FitzGerald Mareno O'Brien	(none)	Rizzuto	Coleman Russo
Trust	Cagney	(none)	Farley Rynne	(none)
Patriot	(none)	(none)	O'Hara Barrone Mercer Murphy	Bartkowicz Goldberg Toreno
Separ	(none)	(none)	Kennedy	Derzon Goldman Hanna Leonard Cohen Kaplan Woodford

Eight officials, the total number in the upper right of Table 7, developed a more separatist self-image, while two respondents, those numbers southwest of the diagonal, became more unionist. Of the twenty officials who originally disagreed with the Supreme Court, 40 per cent inched their way toward the Court's position; one official, or 5 per cent, moved himself into a category more removed from the Court's opinion. One official, who originally was separatist, took a position discrepant from the Court's following the prayer cases.

In Chapter IV I also constructed a measure of the officials' policy preferences in the matter of schoolhouse religion, based on preferences for nine specific religious practices. On the basis of their responses in the initial interviews I classed our twenty-eight educators into four groups, with Group I at one extreme (officials favoring a stigma policy) and Group IV the other (officials wanting an elimination policy). A year later, following *Schempp*, the respondents expressed their preferences for the same nine practices. What changes occurred in the year's time?

Table 9. Policy Preferences of Public School Officials' Attitudes on Schoolhouse Religion before and after *Schempp*

	Group	AFTER: *I* *Stigma*	*II* *Exposure*	*III* *Commonplace*	*IV* *Elimination*	*Total*
BEFORE *Stigma*	*I*	0	0	3	1	4
BEFORE *Exposure*	*II*	2	1	2	1	6
BEFORE *Commonplace*	*III*	1	0	5	1	7
BEFORE *Elimination*	*IV*	1	1	1	8	11
Total		4	2	11	11	28

Non-changers underlined

If the Supreme Court's rule can be said to be an expression of the elimination policy, then those eight officials (29 per cent) in the upper right part of Table 9 reshaped their policy preferences in a direction consonant with the Court's rule, while six (21 per cent) changed in a way discrepant to the Court. If, however, we look only at those seventeen officials originally out of line with the Court's rule, then eight, or 47 per cent, moved toward the Court's policy preference, and only 18 per cent (three officials) magnified an original discrepancy between themselves and the Court.

Table 10. Policy Preferences of Public School Officials' Attitudes on Schoolhouse Religion before and after *Schempp* (by name)

		AFTER:			
	Group	*I*	*II*	*III*	*IV*
BEFORE	*I*	(none)	(none)	Mercer Murphy Barrone	Coleman
	II	FitzGerald Mareno	Berman	Farley Russo	Bartkowicz
	III	Cagney	(none)	Barber Battistella Clancy O'Brien Rynne	Toreno
	IV	O'Hara	Rizzuto	Kennedy	Cohen Derzon Goldberg Goldman Hanna Kaplan Leonard Woodford

A third set of results concerns the equivocation between the self-image and the policy preference of the individual official. In the first round of interviews, before *Schempp,* there existed a high degree of inconsistency between the policy implications of the officials' self-images and their expressed policy preferences. Seventeen of the twenty-eight officials (61 per cent) held self-images at variance with their policy preferences, thirteen having a more, and four a less, religious self-image than would be indicated by their expressed preferences. In the interviews following the prayer cases, only 8 (29 per cent) had equivocal attitudes; five held more and three had less religious feelings/cognitions than their demands for particular practices.

All eight who ended up with equivocation had been originally equivocal, but nine with previously equivocal attitudes (53 per cent)

Table 11. Equivocation between Self-Image and Policy Preferences before and after *Schempp*

		Ethical Measure									
		BEFORE					AFTER				
		UN	TR	PA	SE	TOT	UN	TR	PA	SE	TOT
	I	$\underline{1}$	0	3	0	4	$\underline{3}$	0	1	0	4
	II	4	$\underline{1}$	1	0	6	1	$\underline{0}$	1	0	2
Policy	III	4	2	$\underline{1}$	0	7	4	0	$\underline{6}$	1	11
Measure	IV	1	0	2	$\underline{8}$	11	0	0	0	$\underline{11}$	11
	Totals	10	3	7	8	28	8	0	8	12	28

Unequivocal attitudes underlined

Table 12. Equivocation between Self-Image and Policy Preferences before and after *Schempp* (by name)

		Ethical Measure			
		BEFORE			
		Union	*Trust*	*Patriot*	*Separ*
	I	Coleman	(none)	Barrone Mercer Murphy	(none)
	II	Berman FitzGerald Mareno Russo	Farley	Bartkowicz	(none)
Policy Measure	III	Battistella Barber Clancy O'Brien	Cagney Rynne	Toreno	(none)
	IV	Rizzuto	(none)	O'Hara Goldberg	Derzon Goldman Hanna Leonard Cohen Kaplan Kennedy Woodford

Table 12. Equivocation between Self-Image and Policy Preferences before and after *Schempp* (by name)—*continued*

		AFTER			
	I	Cagney FitzGerald Mareno	(none)	O'Hara	(none)
	II	Berman	(none)	Rizzuto	(none)
Policy Measure	III	Battistella Barber Clancy O'Brien	(none)	Farley Rynne Barrone Mercer Murphy Kennedy	Russo
	IV	(none)	(none)	(none)	Bartkowicz Cohen Kaplan Goldberg Toreno Coleman Derzon Goldman Hanna Leonard Woodford

Table 13. Attitudes toward American Supreme Court, Courts, and Lawyers before and after *Schempp*

	AFTER:					
BEFORE	*Definitely Positive*	*Vaguely Positive*	*Indeterminate*	*Vaguely Negative*	*Definitely Negative*	*Total*
Definitely Positive	6	0	0	0	0	6
Vaguely Positive	2	3	0	0	0	5
Indeterminate	0	1	1	0	1	3
Vaguely Negative	0	5	0	2	3	10
Definitely Negative	0	1	0	0	3	4
Total	8	10	1	2	7	28

Non-changers underlined

brought their policy preferences into coincidence with their self-images. No one with previously consistent attitudes was jarred into equivocation in the year between interviews.

A fourth set of results concerns attitudes toward the Supreme Court. The interviews revealed two kinds of changes: a tendency for attitudes to become more definite and less vague, and a second tendency for them to become more positive and less negative.

Table 14. Attitudes toward American Supreme Court, Courts, and Lawyers before and after *Schempp* (by name)

BEFORE	AFTER: *Definitely Positive*	*Vaguely positive*	*Indeterminate*	*Vaguely negative*	*Definitely Negative*
Definitely positive	Coleman* Goldman Hanna Leonard Barrone* Woodford	(none)	(none)	(none)	(none)
Vaguely positive	Goldberg* Rynne*	Derzon Mercer* Murphy*	(none)	(none)	(none)
Indeterminate	(none)	Toreno*	Kennedy	(none)	Battistella*
Vaguely negative	(none)	Bartkowicz* Cohen Kaplan Rizzuto* Russo*	(none)	Cagney* Farley*	Barber* Clancy* FitzGerald*
Definitely negative	(none)	O'Hara*	(none)	(none)	Berman* Mareno* O'Brien*

*Officials who originally held non-separatist self-images.

The number of officials with definite attitudes increased from ten to fifteen, and with positive attitudes from eleven to eighteen. As to the first tendency, of the six who developed definite attitudes, two ultimately had positive feelings about the Court, and four negative. As to the other tendency, six of the fourteen officials (42 per cent) with originally hostile feelings toward the Court ended up liking it, while none of the eleven officials who originally were attracted to the Court developed a disaffection for it.

Examining the data, I find that twenty officials originally held non-separatist self-images; thus, they had attitudes discrepant from the prayer cases. All six (30 per cent) who originally liked the Court maintained their affection for it. Five more (25 per cent) developed positive feelings where there had been none before. On the other side, seven officials (35 per cent) ended up with a definite dislike for the Court, in contrast to only four who felt deeply hostile toward the Court before *Schempp*.

Table 15. Attitudes toward Supreme Court, etc., before and after *Schempp* among Officials with Originally Non-Separatist Self-Images

	AFTER:					
BEFORE	*Definitely positive*	*Vaguely positive*	*Indeterminate*	*Vaguely negative*	*Definitely negative*	
Definitely positive	2	0	0	0	0	2
Vaguely positive	2	2	0	0	0	4
Indeterminate	0	1	0	0	1	2
Vaguely negative	0	3	0	2	3	8
Definitely negative	0	1	0	0	3	4
Total	4	7	0	2	7	20

Non-changers underlined

To make these figures a little more intelligible, fourteen of the twenty officials who were confronted with an adverse opinion of the Supreme Court actually began with feelings about the Court which at best were non-existent and at worst were hostile. After the adverse decision, five (35 per cent) had been converted to partisans of the Court; another four (30 per cent) became more hostile to the Court; the other five (35 per cent) did not noticeably change their evaluation of the Court —two remaining vaguely negative, and three definitely negative.

If there is any one point to be made from all these many data, it is this: within any single discreet organization of individuals whose behavior lawmakers intend to affect, the reaction to the law is never monolithic within the group but varies from person to person. The responses do not move in the same direction, nor with the same intensity, nor with respect to the same objects. It was this varied range of response which was the most important result of my study, and explanation of these variabilities is my most important task.

The Control Group

None of these data establishes conclusively that the Supreme Court decision caused any of these attitude changes, although the respondents themselves, in their various interviews, repeatedly mentioned the importance of the prayer cases in heightening their feelings about the Court and in shaping up their attitudes toward religious practices.

Some further evidence exists to corroborate my theory that the Supreme Court decision was causally linked to the attitude changes just recorded.

Between interviews a year or more passed, and a momentous year it was. There were the assassination of President Kennedy, the civil rights march in Washington, the violence of the white Southern defense, the appearance of the so-called white backlash. Abroad, the war in Vietnam enlarged, the rift widened between Russia and China, and there was a dramatic confrontation of Russia and the United States in Cuba. In the religious realm, Pope John died, Pope Paul was elected, and the Ecumenical Council met in Rome. In domestic politics, there were mounting intensity in the debate on governmental aid to parochial schools and increased visibility of the churches' involvement in the cause of civil rights. On the economic front, Presidents Kennedy and Johnson eloquently contrasted America's affluence with the poverty of insular minorities throughout the United States. And in Midland affairs, there were the mayoralty election, resignations and appointments in the educational system, and the preparation of a program to eliminate racial imbalance from the schools. For each of the twenty-eight officials, there were private tragedies and public triumphs, job changes, new problems, and new acquaintances.

The changes of attitudes that have been tabulated could conceivably have been the result of a variety of causes, or even of a single non-legal factor.

To check this possibility, interviews before and after the Supreme Court's prayer decision were conducted with the headmasters of the five Midland private secular schools. These headmasters were all Protestant; their school populations, for the most part racially and religiously mixed, were more white Protestant and well-to-do than Midland students generally. The headmasters had been educated at more prestigious colleges than public school principals and were more widely traveled, although they tended to have less graduate school experience.

In most respects similarities existed. Politically, the headmasters were a mixture of conservatives and liberals (as were the public school principals), and they seemed as removed from partisan politics (two were registered Republicans). They were exposed to much the same political, religious, and economic pressures as public school educators; and while Midland politics may not have had so intimate a bearing on their school policies and salary scales, they were still Midland citizens, living within the city and very much touched by the fiscal and social policies of the municipal government.

One distinction between the situation of the twenty-eight public school officials and the five private school headmasters was the impact of the law of the *Schempp* case. Because the Fourteenth Amendment does not apply to persons in private employ but only to officials who are state agents, the private schools in Midland and elsewhere were not touched by the prayer ban. Midland headmasters were free to continue religious traditions in their schools if they wished.

The interviews with the private officials were abbreviated, but in both the before and after interviews there were included the nine questions comprising the measure of policy preferences on schoolhouse religion. Thus, there were pre- and post-decision policy measures for both public and private officials, for persons whom the law affected and for persons whom the law did not.

In their original attitudes about religious practices (as measured by the policy measure), the private school headmasters tended to be slightly more predisposed to devotional practices in the classroom. Three ranked in Group I (the stigma policy) one in Group II (the exposure policy), and only one urged an elimination policy. (In fact, the actual religious practices in the private schools tended to be more extensive also.) Yet both groups of educators represented a fairly wide spectrum of attitudes.

How did their post-*Schempp* changes in policy preferences compare? Among the public school officials, fifteen, or 54 per cent, shifted their preferences one way or the other between interviews. Among the private school headmasters, not one shifted his preferences during the year. Looking only at those seventeen public and four private school officials with original preferences inconsistent with the Supreme Court's rule on prayers, I got the result in Table 16.

Table 16. Changes in the Policy Measure of Their Attitudes among Public and Private School Officials Originally Discrepant with the Prayer Decision

	Change	*No Change*	*Total*
Private Official	0	4	4
Public Official	11	6	17
Totals	11	10	21

All the momentous events of 1963, except the prayer decision, jarred private and public officials alike. Yet, on the matter of schoolhouse religion, only the public school officials shifted their moorings. The law (or rather the events which the Court's ruling initiated) seems to have been a necessary causal factor in inducing changes of attitude in public school personnel.

Theoretical Recapitulation

Chapter I set forth four different effects which acute observers have attributed to law when it clashed with men's attitudes. I called these the nulist, the backlash, the conversion, and the liberating effects. In addition, I catalogued an additional four possible reactions to an adverse legal message—denial, wishful interpretation, indecision, and leaving the legal field altogether. Furthermore, Chapter I suggested that all eight reactions were plausibly predicted within the theoretical framework of cognitive dissonance research—namely, that adverse law presents an individual with a choice, the resolution of which begets a post mortem dissonance that has to be discharged.

My study revealed a wide variety of response to the prayer decision among the twenty-eight respondents. Four backlashed (Mareno, Miss FitzGerald, Cagney, and Berman). In the face of a law critical of prayers in the public schools, each developed a more favorable attitude toward schoolhouse religion (on either the self-image or preference measures or both). Four were nulists (Clancy, Miss Barber, Miss Battistella, and Miss O'Brien); they remained neither more nor less favorable than their originally favorable attitudes. There were five who showed the conversion effect (Coleman, Dr. Bartkowicz, Russo, Mrs. Goldberg, and Mrs. Toreno); each became critical of schoolhouse religion (on one or both of the measures) where before they had been favorable. There were five persons who showed the liberative effect (Miss Barrone, Farley, Miss Mercer, Murphy, and Rynne); each developed less favorable attitudes (although not critical ones) on either the self-image or policy-preference measures or both. In addition, there were two other groups of officials, those whose original attitudes were critical of schoolhouse religion. There were the seven vindicateds (Derzon, Goldman, Mrs. Hanna, Leonard, Miss Cohen, Kaplan, and Woodford), whose attitudes remained critical. And lastly, there were the reverse liberateds (Rizzuto, Miss O'Hara, and Miss Kennedy), whose originally critical feelings toward schoolhouse religion (on one or both measures) became favorable in the face of a law denigrating it. Of these six groups, only the backlashers and the nulists derogated the Supreme Court; the remaining four groups tended to raise the Court in their esteem.[2]

Why did one individual choose one reaction, and another a different avenue?

The Backlashers

Cagney, Miss FitzGerald, Mareno and Berman developed more favorable attitudes toward schoolhouse religion.

Each of the four backlashers intensified his attitudes about the importance of religion in the schoolroom; none acknowledged the bad effects of religious practices or the good effects of the prayer ban.

The backlashers surreptitiously introduced religious ceremony into the curriculum through whatever loopholes they could find in the prayer ban—the Christmas skit, the Easter play, the special occasion. Berman, for example, said: "During graduation assembly, in addition to reading the Bible, I read one prayer of Mary Stuart. There is a lot

[2] There may well be some dispute as to the placement of Berman among the backlashers and Mrs. Goldberg among the converts. Berman closely resembles the nulist (he became neither more nor less favorable on the self-image and policy-preference measures); he differs from them, however, on the greater extent of practices which he preferred. As for Mrs. Goldberg, although she rated in Group IV on the policy-preference measure in the original interview, she expressed at that time a strong preference for classroom prayers which, in her case, received no weight by virtue of the cumulative modification of the Guttman scale employed. This preference disappeared in the second interview.

of guidance in that message; so I read it as a piece of guidance, and didn't even call it a prayer. I got around the ban, and I felt a lot better." The backlashers refused to recognize the rationale behind the ban. None except Berman could give an explanation of why the Court decided the way it did.

In contrast, each thirsted for information and social support which would strengthen their opinion of the Court as cheapened, ignored, and a pay-off thing. The best illustration of this process of selective search occurred accidentally as Berman and I left a drugstore where we had lunched together. A Republican party volunteer passed by carrying literature on Senator Barry Goldwater's criticism of the Court. Berman reached out avidly for it and commented, "This is what I have been waiting for"—psychic ammunition. The backlashers were well committed to resist the Court actively and to defy the ban in their hearts.

Why was resistance to the Court more attractive than other alternatives? For example, what was so repulsive about choosing to comply with the Court?

For one thing, all started with a negative attitude toward the Supreme Court before the prayer cases. To have complied with the Court would have required some mental adjustments. Mareno, for example, was comfortable when the Supreme Court (which he disliked) prohibited prayers (which he liked). Had he conformed to the Court's rule, he would have been in the position where he was committed to wanting the same action the despised Court wanted. To find yourself, as Mareno would have, in cahoots with an enemy is always a bit disturbing. Yet, at least one of the backlashers—Cagney—began with an attitude toward the Court so vague as to be negligible. It is necessary to find some explanation other than an initial animosity to the Court.

Clearly, there were costs in accepting the premises of *Schempp*. We have spoken of the anchor which religious life provided Miss FitzGerald's existence. The Court decision struck at those very concepts which made her life comprehensible. To her a philosophy in which God could be separated from the learning of worldly wisdom was self-contradictory. Her single measure of self-esteem, the provision to children of a God theory of reality, was attacked by the Court's opinion. Acceptance of the Court's separatist concept meant so many far-reaching repercussions and posed such a threat to her dignity that she had to resist.

For Mareno and Cagney, compliance would have jeopardized important friendships. Both these men had chosen to remove themselves from the social circles of Midland's public school educators. On a Social Activities Index measuring involvement in the social life within the school system, scaling from zero to four,[3] only four principals scored less than two. Mareno and Cagney both scored zero. Their social lives were in the larger Midland community, amidst people whose own attitudes were uncompromisingly hostile to the Court's. To accept the Court's opinion was to make the two men unattractive socially; resistance made them heroes. The Rotary Club, of which Mareno was a member, was hardly likely to praise him for knuckling under to the prayer ban.[4] Cagney, an active member of the Knights of Columbus, found it similarly unattractive to take a single-handed stand in favor of the prayer ban.

The interesting fact is that the backlashers made no attempt to reduce the importance of schoolhouse religion; they did not vitiate the instrumental link between it and character building. On the contrary, they made it even more exclusive a determinant of morals and its absence from the schools even more disastrous an event. As Mareno put it for all four, "The requirement of the Supreme Court will weaken the fabric of our country."

Immediately after the school board announced the prayer ban, Dr. Bartkowicz and Goldman suggested the formation of a lay-staff committee to enrich the curriculum with moral and ethical values. At the time of the second interview a few meetings of the committee had already been held; suggestions had been elicited from the staff; but the project had hardly left the ground. No backlasher had made a contribution to the committee. Furthermore, to a man they denied that the

[3] See Appendix for method of constructing the Index.

[4] Suppose, for example, that the president of Rotary had called on Mareno impromptu to make a few remarks at the weekly luncheon on the school board's prayer ban. It is worth speculating that the Rotarian character of the audience at Mareno's maiden public remarks about the ban affected his commitment against the Court. See a stimulating article by R. A. Bauer, "The Communicator and the Audience," *Journal of Conflict Resolution,* 2 (1958), 67-77, in which the author remarks at one point: "A person might never formulate his impressions . . . until he was in the position of having to communicate them to someone else. In this event, the first audience to whom he addressed himself would influence the way in which he would organize his information and the terms in which he would couch his conclusions. In this way the audience would influence what he would later remember and believe."

committee ever would have an effect on character development. Especially was this so of Berman, who said: "Nothing has happened. That idea was just a lot of talk . . . like every other program Bartkowicz has tried to put through." Bartkowicz's role in the prayer ban may explain Berman's reluctance to reduce the intensity of his original attitude. Were he to reduce the discrepancy between him and the law by admitting the possible usefulness of a non-religious means of character development, he would run head on into the belief that everything which Bartkowicz ("I couldn't stand him") tried to put through was worthless. Complying with a ban Dr. Bartkowicz had helped promulgate raised more psychological problems than it solved.

Similarly, the other three, while not explicit in their disaffection for Bartkowicz, voiced real dissatisfaction with the superintendent'es educational policies. Berman, Mareno, Cagney, and Miss FitzGerald were, in short, demoralized: with Bartkowicz at the helm of the system, they were no longer willing to make unsolicited contributions to the school organization. Nor were they any longer willing to make accommodation to things personally unpleasant. It was not the prayer ban that created the discontent; rather, the changes in philosophy of the school system, which accompanied Bartkowicz's advent, had made the educational system more of a burden than a reward for these four. They had taken Bartkowicz's assertion of changes as an implied rebuke to themselves.

To these four demoralized officials, submitting to the Court's prayer decision was hardly a matter of indifference. Once it had the support of the disliked superintendent, compliance with the law was submission to him—and that was a denigration of themselves.

One alternative for these four was to leave the school system. As a matter of fact, Mareno did resign within a month of our last interview, leaving a job which he had described earlier (and before Bartkowicz's presence had been strongly felt) as "one of the most rewarding experiences a man could have." For the others, quitting was an available alternative. Miss FitzGerald was "not going to stay about" unless prayers were restored. Even with all the dislocation entailed in quitting an organization at a time when so much personal investment had been made in it, leaving the field of choice was not beyond the possibility for these disaffected.

The very fact that all four had considered the possibility of revoking their commitment to the system foreclosed one other possible response. I have mentioned the fact that one alternative was to deny that there was really a choice: typically, the individual could exaggerate the sanctions so that he perceived himself acting without any volition. For those, however, for whom quitting was a viable alternative, the element of volition remained prominent, leaving the anxiety of choice undiminished. The result was that they accentuated their original attitudes. For these four—but for these alone—defiance of the law became the easiest course, so long as they chose to remain within the Midland public school organization.

The Nulists

Clancy, Miss Barber, Miss Battistella, and Miss O'Brien remained neither more nor less favorable toward schoolhouse religion.

The identifying characteristic of the nulist was that neither his self-image nor his expressed policy preferences on schoolhouse religious practices changed in the two interviews, even though his attitude was extremely equivocal. Each nulist remained unionist in self-image, and each retained his watered-down policy preference for merely the commonplace religious exercises. Unlike the backlasher, the nulist had committed himself, not to defy the law, but to conform to it. Three—all except Miss O'Brien—were tuned into the Court's message; to varying degrees they "knew [that the Court was] worried about the people who did not believe in the Lord's Prayer."

Having received the Court's message, the nulist began to recognize certain unhappy consequences of previous policies ("My Jewish friends tell me they did not like prayer") and some positive attributes of the prayer ban ("There has been an emphasis on patriotism and patriotic songs"). Nonetheless, for the nulist, the connection between schoolhouse religion and character development seemed to be as intense as it did originally.

Why did these officials tolerate the inconsistency between the implications of their unionist self-image and their expressed preferences for so little schoolhouse religion? In the case of three nulists—all but Miss O'Brien—the answer came most revealingly in Clancy's description of how "I called up the chancery [the archdiocese of the state] and asked them what I should do as a good Catholic. They said I had no alternative but to go along with the Court." With no alternative available, Clancy's compliance was not a matter of volition. To reassure himself of his lack of choice he sought testimonials from the chancery and from Goldman, whose skill in briefing the board and the public on the ineluctability of the Court's mandate he much appreciated. Goldman presented an invulnerable case, precluding choice, obviating an effort to interpret the decision.

Dr. Clancy, Miss Barber, and Miss Battistella had no choice to make. They behaved involuntarily. The ban was not their responsibility.

Contrast the nulists' behavior with the backlashers'. Instead of defying the spirit of the law, the nulists scrupulously, almost militantly, hewed to the letter of it, as if their lives depended on it. Miss Barber would not allow silent prayer in her school, because the prayer ban did not explicitly approve it. After the prayer ban she never mentioned God in any of her personal counseling, not even when talking to the child of a Protestant minister. She permitted no prayers at the time of President Kennedy's assassination. She even refrained from disabusing a teacher of the idea that the ban on schoolhouse religion forbade teaching the Golden Rule.

Dr. Clancy was more sophisticated; he differentiated between religion and philosophy, but the line between them was impassably rigid. The law was the law, and the nulists were bound to stay within it, shying away from the margins as if hell lay just the other side.

To these three the Supreme Court was perceived as having "tremendous power," as being "important," as "exerting a lot of pressure," as expressing the public will. The Court controlled the official's destiny and his discretion. The more powerful the Court, the less volition "we" had. The more overwhelmed the teaching staff, the less responsibility did it share for its behavior. When the nulist built up the Court's irresistibility, he fortified his own self-esteem; when he acquiesced, he wanted to do it to an invincible opponent. The more invulnerable Goldman's legal opinion to loopholes, the less damning the nulist's conformity to the law.

This tendency to exaggerate the power of the Court was not without its unsettling implications. For example, to Miss Battistella the Court seemed so formidable that she began to worry about the dangers such power posed for American democracy. By and large, however, exaggeration of the Court's invincibility was a simple solution.

Why was resistance to the Court's decision unattractive to the nulists when it was such an easy alternative for the backlashers? One answer was that all three—Miss Battistella, Miss Barber, and Dr. Clancy—enjoyed the social contact which the Midland school system gave them. All three wished to maintain the harmonious relationships which existed among the professional staff and among the school board. They had an interest in toning down their differences, in becoming indifferent, over matters which divided and caused unpleasantnesses. Miss Barber expressed her distaste for antagonism within the school system. Miss Battistella, inextricably bound up in innumerable committees, was frightened of factions. Dr. Clancy, exalted by the companionship of his six important colleagues on the board, was frightened that the more articulate Leonard and the eloquent Goldman would make a fool of him if the debate got acrimonious.

The communities on which these three depended for friendship and support did not want these three persons to resist. Their friends had a stake in the Midland public school system, and resistance which led to dissension was clearly counter-productive, and that would not have been good.

They remained silent, bearing the inconsistency between their religious self-image and their meager policy preferences by thinking themselves into the position where they had no choice. They accommodated the needs of the organization yet retained their original attitudes. The nulist was the true equivocator.

But why was attitudinal compliance unattractive? Why did they not change their feelings and their cognitions? Compliance, for these three, was not so unattractive as it was intellectually impossible. These three lacked the ability to rationalize opinion change. I have spoken of Dr. Clancy's inarticulateness. I have previously noted Miss Battistella's difficulties in tolerating change because of her inability to distinguish important from unimportant repercussions. Now I can speak of Miss Barber.

Miss Barber was a veritable communications sponge. She listened to everybody: her teachers, her student teachers, a woman judge she knew, her sisters, her agnostic nephew, a cousin who was a lawyer, the state commissioner of education, the custodian in her school. She said of herself, "I listen to discussions at parties." She "read anything that I can get on the Court," with no differentiation between pro and con. For example, she spoke approvingly of virulent anti-Court propaganda and then mentioned in the same breath an article lauding the Court. She was sent articles by her brother-in-law, she clipped others on her own, and then she kept them on file at home. The concepts and the ideas in those articles went into the file but never integrated themselves into Miss Barber's mind.

She habitually introduced details into her answers which were invariably inaccurate: Franklin D. Roosevelt had tried to pack the

Court with fourteen justices; separate but equal school facilities was the present law of the land; she confused Justice Potter Stewart with Justice William Douglas. Everything was "kind of vague," as she once said of her impression of the Court.

Miss Barber compounded the problem of her unselective listening habits by a reticence which denied her the chance to air the vague mass of opinion and feelings cluttering up her head. She indicated her frustration at being inarticulate at crucial moments: "At the meeting where we were told the policy (by Goldman) . . . no one dared to stand up and object. One or two voiced disagreement . . . but no one else did. We just went ahead and took our directions."

Lacking the courage to argue, Miss Barber lost her chance to clarify her own thinking. Dr. Clancy and Miss Battistella were troubled in the same way as Miss Barber. These three never could work the unfamiliar concepts of pluralism and separatism into their own attitude structures securely enough to withstand the rebuke of others. One has to imagine Clancy sitting and listening to the extensive debate within the school board meetings, inventorying all the separatists' ammunition Goldman, Leonard, Mrs. Hanna, and Rizzuto developed, but always remaining silent. As Goldman said, "Clancy is such a quiet guy." Then, after the meeting Clancy would go back to a world where friends accosted him and accused him, and—not quite sure what those separatist arguments would sound like in his mouth, not quite confident in his abilities to withstand a social assault, not quite comprehending the implications and limits of the separatist ideas he had been provisioned with, not practiced in the weaponry he carried—he would not defend himself. He would retreat ignominiously, apologetically, saying: "It's not our decision; it's the law of the land, and we have to go along with it."

Dr. Clancy, Miss Barber, and Miss Battistella, for intellectual reasons, were never able to smooth things out in their own thinking. So they found the easiest solution was to rule out choice, by exaggerating the Court's omnipotence.

The quiet but redoubtable Molly O'Brien resembled these three only in the unchangeability of her originally equivocal attitude. Unlike Dr. Clancy, Miss Barber, and Miss Battistella, however, she paid little attention to the Court; she did not admit any good attributes to the prayer ban; she did not hew to the letter of the law with militant rigidity; she did not attribute omnipotence to the Court, and she was not concerned about continuing harmonious social relations within the system. Her principal social activity was now her Catholic charity work. In these ways she differed from the other three nulists.

She did not, however, have the characteristics of the typical backlasher. She did not increase her preferences for religious practices. She was not repelled by the thought of the Court (even though she had originally a definitely negative response to it.) She was even willing to admit the dangers of teachers' abuse of schoolhouse religion. How then did she deal with the nulist inconsistency between her attitudes and her commitment to conform overtly?

I think the answer lay in her age, that she was, as she put it, "another generation." Miss O'Brien, as she approached retirement, had begun to cut up history into generations; hers had completed its responsibility of reproducing and cultivating its successor. It was not her world to guide any more. It was the Supreme Court of the next generation that had decided against religion in schools, and, as she said, prayer "may not be right now," any more than the adventurous and aggressive business practices of her generation were necessarily appropriate in the 1960's. She wanted to avoid conflict; she wanted her past and her accomplishments judged, not in the light of today's advantages, knowledge, and values, but in the light of the difficulties, limitations, and ideals of her day. Any other judgment was an ahistorical post mortem.

Therefore, it was annoying for Goldman and the law to condemn, if only by implication, what her generation of teachers had done. Let Goldman and his generation have their way today, but do not judge us—that was the message which lay between the lines of this parting shot at Goldman:

> There was something else Mr. Goldman said that annoyed me. He said: "Having children say prayers they didn't believe in was comparable to putting all the little Negro children out in the hall and saying, 'I'm not going to tell you about your lesson, just the other children.' " There just is no analogy there. That's not piety; that's injustice. To me it meant nothing. It was ridiculous, and I found it annoying.

Why was it so annoying? Because, in Miss O'Brien's estimate, the contribution of her generation had been the recognition of the occurrence of racial injustice. In her time the Negro was made inherently equal; in her time her beloved mother Church had embraced the colored race; in her time the Negro began his assimilation into American life. Measured in terms of the starting point from which the Negro began when Miss O'Brien's generation took responsibility, racial progress had been monumental, and now Goldman was imputing to her generation an uncompassionate heart.

Miss O'Brien was too old to dissociate herself or to start building identifications with new organizations, as the detached Mareno might have done. Those thousands of students who had previously fallen within her intimate Catholic influence had done well, given the hard circumstances in which they found themselves at the beginning. In her retirement Miss O'Brien wanted to preserve untainted her memories of those children grown mature. Any imputation that her accomplishments had been insufficient was unacceptable. At the same time, she did not have the energy to make the fight. She was retreating from the field in two years; if she could temporize for that brief time, then she could live out her imminent solitude with her memories of "my life—and a wonderful life."

The Converts

Coleman, Dr. Bartkowicz, Russo, Mrs. Toreno and Mrs. Goldberg became critical of schoolhouse religion where they had originally been favorable.

The converts became committed to eliminating schoolhouse religion as a result of the prayer decision. They became separatist, where they were once non-separatist. They developed a skepticism about schoolhouse religion as being either necessary or sufficient to build character of schoolchildren. Where they had tended to be negative in their feelings about the Supreme Court, they ended with an affection for it. These five were the converts of the law.

The changes in their attitudes varied from the extensive to the barely perceptible. Bartkowicz's denigration of collective prayer, you will remember, was striking. So was the contrast between the outspoken Russo's cognition of the relationship between religion and morals ("Morals have got to have a religious basis"—pre-*Schempp;* "Morals do not boil down to one thing; they boil down to a combination of little things"—post-*Schempp.*) Coleman now saw that "kids . . . don't get anything out of" the ritual of prayer, where before it had meant so "much [when] you're in trouble." Mrs. Toreno's view of religious heterogeneity changed less dramatically, but the alteration was still visible. At her first interview: "Only the little [religions] are basically different, and here the question is, must the majority submit to the minority?" At her second interview: "If the children were being hurt, even if it was only a few children of minority groups, I'm glad we have avoided that now."

Interestingly enough, the more unionist the converted official before *Schempp,* the more separatist was he afterward. Mrs. Goldberg, nearly separatist in the period before the prayer ban, still longed for "a little bit of religion," but not so the former unionists Russo and Coleman.

In the previous section I remarked how the nulist emphasized his lack of volition in conforming to the prayer ban. He had no alternative but to go along with the law. In contrast, the converts strongly asserted their freedom of choice between the alternatives of compliance and defiance. Dr. Bartkowicz, for instance, complied with *Schempp* because it "is our responsibility for holding up and respecting the law, even though there is no reason in the world to think that the Court will enforce this." Even Russo, who as a principal had no hand in formulating board policy, asserted his intellectual freedom in agreeing with the prayer ban by insisting that *Schempp* did not require the ban; but: "There is a point where one on the basis of principle and intellect should go one step beyond what is ordered, to do the right way."

Why did these officials emphasize their choice in accepting the law? Volition transformed a legal necessity into a moral virtue. Mrs. Toreno slept soundly, knowing that she had preserved a minority group child from being hurt; in contrast, Miss Barber, the nulist, introspectively wondered whether her hesitation in mentioning God to a small child had been cowardice. Volition made personal action in accordance with the law a credit to Mrs. Toreno's self-esteem, but coercion demeaned the same behavior of Miss Barber. Volition was attractive because it provided the psychological rewards of personal responsibility.

Furthermore, volition made the individual free to act as he thought right. Remember how the nulist rigidly clamped the letter of the law on his own spontaneous reactions. In contrast, the converts exercised a notable freedom from anxiety in allowing religious occasions in his school. He felt comfortable exercising discretion. Dr. Bartkowicz permitted the singing of Christmas carols, "even carols with a strong religious theme." Russo and Mrs. Toreno had no qualms about letting the students pray when "it is appropriate to pray" (e.g., at the news of President Kennedy's assassination). The spontaneity of the converts in permitting religiously tinged observances contrasted with the nulist self-conciousness in permitting the same activities. The convert acted with assurance; the nulist was full of self-doubt.

If emphasis on volition had its rewards in terms of self-esteem, it also had its costs. Volition compelled the individual to modify his attitudes. This alteration was neither easy nor without risks to intellectual stability. The convert might overreact, as Coleman did, "may overestimate change from one extreme to another."[5]

Coleman began with the opinion that classroom prayer (which he liked) aided Negro assimilation into white culture (which he liked). When the Supreme Court (which he also liked) banned religion from the public schools, he had to choose between prayer and the Court, two well-liked alternatives.

If he had wished, he might have emphasized his own compulsion (or, going one step further back, the Court's lack of constitutional choice) in prohibiting religion, thereby eliminating the dissonance, but at the same time denying his volition. On the other hand, he could (and ultimately did) emphasize his freedom to comply. Coleman thereby made attitude change necessary. He found it impossible to alter his feelings about the Supreme Court. "I wasn't as interested in the problem of [religion] as in de facto segregation," and de facto segregation "revert[ed] back to the Court." At the same time, he had considerable difficulty in denying that religion assisted Negroes. (In my earlier discussion I mentioned Coleman's personal experience of oneness with whites derived from learning a common cultural heritage.)

His solution was to differentiate[6] between religion in general (which he continued to regard as assimilationist) and religion as taught by public school teachers (which he regarded as racially divisive). He then focused the Court's condemnation upon the public school teachers; he converted his previously impossible choice between prayers or the Court into an easy one between compliance (which he liked) and teachers' dogmatism (which he disliked). To reinforce the distinction between religion and dogmatism, Coleman searched for informational support. He soon developed a generalization that any valuable program was likely to be corrupted by Midland teachers, whether it were ethical training, college counseling, or personal advice. This generalization was a sharp modification of a previously ambivalent image of teachers (while some "take off to the moon," others have real imagination). He now stigmatized all teachers as weak, a "bunch of cream puffs,"

[5] *Brehm and Cohen,* p. 106.

[6] Milton J. Rosenberg, *et al., Attitude Organization and Change* (New Haven: Yale University Press, 1960), p. 34.

who forced "their own anxieties onto our children" and then "closed the day by beating the kids out of the classroom door." Alas, this unfavorable picture of teachers, while supporting the religious differentiation, proved too much, for the Midland school child was left (in the mind of Coleman) in the hands of miserable teachers with little chance of getting a decent cultural background. He admitted to himself that this sad state of things hardly redounded to the credit of the school board. In short, his meddling with his original attitude structure put a painful wrinkle into his own self-esteem.

Coleman's solution was to see that the teachers would be improved by the prayer ban in the long run, that "the board by standing up and being counted, and by relieving the teachers of some of their indecision, may make them stronger teachers." There was not much conviction behind this wishful observation; Coleman conceded: "Maybe I'm trying to smooth something over in my own thinking."

Notice how he attempted to smooth out his thinking. He asserted that while harm might result from the board's ban of prayers in the short run, its long-term consequence would be to bring about the improvement of the teaching staff (who in turn would speed Negro assimilation). This intellectual device of extending one's time perspective to more indirect repercussions in the future was an extremely common intellectutal device among the twenty-eight respondents. The device bore a close kinship to the phenomenon of sour grapes. A person who is sour grapes is one who admits that while things are working fine right now, the consequence in the future is bound to be dreadful. Coleman (and almost every official who changed his attitudes) used reverse sour grapes (the psychologist Rosenberg found it so common, he gave the technique the name sweet lemons).[7] Coleman looked past unfavorable short-range repercussions and emphasized the long-range good of his commitment.

I detailed Coleman's intellectual efforts because his story illustrated the domino effect of tampering with attitudes: a change in a belief about prayer impinged on its neighbors about teachers and about personal self-esteem. The description also illustrated two important intellectual tools of attitude change, differentiation, and sweet lemons. Notice one more fact: Coleman manipulated the reality concerning character development; where he had once thought that religion increased Negro assimilation, he later believed exactly the opposite. He changed his theory of character formation, and what enabled him

[7] *Ibid.*, p. 35.

to be so intellectually irresponsible was the fact that in Midland there was no agreement that any one theory of character formation was much truer than some other. Some realities would of course not be so fuzzy; some facts might be so bolted down that they would resist wishful distortion, putting much greater limitations on dealing with the repercussions of cutting out old attitudes. For instance, it would have been nearly impossible for Coleman to have altered the fact that the Supreme Court had prohibited religious exercises, what with Goldman telling him otherwise and threatening a lawsuit to prove it. Coleman would not have been free to shape this fact according to some hope of his, in which case he might have had to forgo converting old attitudes and resorted, as did the nulist, to emphasizing the element of coercion in his conforming to the Court.

Motivation to change attitudes was one thing; ability to do so was another matter, as the nulists found out. I have said of three of the nulists (Dr. Clancy, Miss Barber, and Miss Battistella) that they were incapable of attitude change. They were unable to learn their new attitudes well enough to defend themselves against the social retaliations inflicted on them. The converts could change, because they were articulate, or because they lived in a less hostile reality, or for both reasons. Mrs. Goldberg, a woman who shunned controversy, told how persons would tell her "it was too bad we had to be told what we could do with our religion in a country where there was freedom of religion." But where the nulist failed this kind of social test, Mrs. Goldberg would concisely reply: "Freedom of religion was the very essence of the Supreme Court's decision, and they had decided that way to keep children from being forced to be religious in a way opposed to their own religion." Successful rebuttal in everyday social debate separated the converts from the nulists.

To be successfully articulate was not easy. It took energy for the individual official to convince himself; it took homework; and it took time to become aware of the subtle implications of the new attitudes. Dr. Bartkowicz, the New Dealer, had to remedy his long-standing antipathy to the Court arising out of his identification with F.D.R., and he did so by reading Alexander Bickel's *The Least Dangerous Branch*. Russo read the National Education Association materials on the prayer decision—"When the Court came down with this decision, which was opposite my own, I began to do some reading on the subject on my own."

Sometimes the sources drawn on were previously internalized.

Coleman merely tapped a reservoir of knowledge about the Court, built up with respect to the desegregation cases a decade ago. However, he only began to tap the information filed away under desegregation after Goldman had pointed out the parallels between non-compliance with the prayer cases and the Southern resistance to desegregation. When Goldman made the connection for him, Coleman found his ammunition.

In Mrs. Toreno and Mrs. Goldberg, two officials who started with more separatist attitudes than the three men did, the transition that was required was not very great. A slight difference in emphasis, as small as necessary to accomplish the commitment, was not very laborious.

As to the factor of social hostility which these five converts met when they changed their attitudes—and this fact is striking—the proving ground on which their eloquence was tested was much less treacherous than the three nulists found. The five converted officials were not obligated to persons interested in maintaining schoolhouse religion. All three principals had just come to their respective schools at the time of the first interview. As a result, they were working with a staff which hardly knew them and had no expectations for them on the subject of prayers. The same was true for their P.T.A.'s. The three had no past commitments to schoolhouse religion which had to be lived down.

Coleman and Dr. Bartkowicz, at higher positions in the school system, were also detached. The solitary Bartkowicz, purposefully having eschewed social connections, had to loose few bonds of friendship, because he had few friends. Coleman, a newcomer to town, knew hardly any Catholics; he circulated within a racially circumscribed community which was little bothered by the issue.

The social relationships of the converts were simplicity itself. They were not prisoners of the community in which they worked. They had no past to reconcile with their new commitment to separatism. So far as their communities were concerned, the people had no specific set of "oughts" derived from long-standing practice that now had to be defied or redefined. When a man need not explain why he is a turncoat, the task of attitude change is markedly easier.

We might ask why resistance to the Court was less attractive to the converts than attitudinal compliance? What distinguished them from the backlashers?

First, they did not have time to resist. Each of the five had on his agenda matters that had priority over schoolhouse religion. Mrs. Goldberg had a sick husband and mother. Mrs. Toreno had a new school, which was Midland's showpiece and involved her in a great many time-consuming ceremonial duties. Russo had just been made a principal and, in addition to learning the ropes of his new job, was deeply involved as the liaison between the local teachers' association and the state department of education. Bartkowicz and Coleman were worried about implementing the controversial racial imbalance program. Being out of step with the law on prayers took time, drained energy, preoccupied psychic space, and exposed them to attacks from the "nuts." They wanted to free themselves for more important problems. At the moment they were overcommitted. (Religion meant much to these five persons, but other events had crowded religious concerns off stage center.)

In contrast the backlashers had no stake in remedying racial imbalance. They had no potential future prestige that would not be realized if the school system were damaged. They were veteran principals who had their jobs under control. There was time to spare.

Second, these five were happy with the system, not demoralized. Their work within the organization was profitable, not burdensome. Mrs. Goldberg's new principalship meant a paycheck to meet hospital bills, and it obliged her to stop thinking about the illnesses of people she loved. Mrs. Toreno obtained prestige from showing her new school to the upper officialdom of Midland and to educational experts from the world over. Opportunities for the youthful Russo in the Midland and state systems beckoned. As the first Negro to be elevated to the school board, Coleman was in the political limelight constantly. Bartkowicz understood that the Midland system posed a sufficiently complex problem in which to prove his courage, skills, and merits to school boards in larger cities which might be looking for a new superintendent. An organization as productive as Midland's was to these five could make severe demands and still obtain compliance.

At the same time, their history of non-commitment to their educational colleagues left these five converted educators without personal influence among the staff and parents. They had no status as friends, no store of credits built up by a series of small favors done. They carried no weight. They were company men, and their conversion to separatism, while socially easy, had at best little persuasive effect on the veterans of the system; at worst, it may have been repulsive.

The Liberateds

Miss Barrone, Farley, Miss Mercer, Murphy, and Rynne developed less favorable attitudes toward schoolhouse religion but not critical ones.

The liberateds were veteran Midland educators. All born and raised in Midland, all members of the system for at least twenty years, they were actively involved in the formal and informal social life of the system. Four scaled four on the Social Activities Index, on which four was the most active, and the fifth, Farley, scaled three. They were all Catholic and devout, and all administered schools which were attended by few Jewish students. Each had been principal at his particular school for more than five years (except Rynne, who was transferred from one junior high school to another between interviews). They intimately knew their staff, and they had a reputation in their neighborhoods.

Common to four of the five was the elimination of the original inconsistency between their self-image and expressed policy preferences, always in a direction consistent with the Court's decision. Miss Barrone, Miss Mercer, and Murphy began with a patriot self-image and a stigma (Group I) policy preference; after the prayer decision their policy preferences changed to Group III. Conversely, Rynne trimmed his trustee self-concept to fit his original Group III preferences; he became a patriot.

They were each bound up in the public school organization. Murphy was past president of the teachers' association—Rynne was his successor. Farley organized an American Federation of Teachers chapter to rival the teachers' association but maintained an active role in both groups. The two women had become increasingly active in the Principals' Club.

They were bound, not only to the school system, but to their neighborhoods in which their schools were situated. They were part of the community. As Miss Mercer put it, "They bring their personal problems to me." Miss Barrone was a member of the Community Council of her neighborhood. Murphy, rooted in a very stable lower–middle-class neighborhood, was teaching children of children he had taught a generation ago. Farley and Rynne, the politicians, searched out the feelings of the people. For these five, the complexity of their obligations was great, and the assigning of priorities among them was invariably problematical. As Farley put it, "It's hard to separate a personal reaction from a professional reaction." For him, he was both a member of an educational organization and also a servant of the neighborhood, even though the codes of each might be completely incompatible.

They refrained from being unequivocal company men, not out of disloyalty to the school system, but because each was a "localist," as Rynne said, who had to work for the best of his community as well as to serve the system. These were persons in constant attitudinal conflict, who were used to the conflict between the part and the whole, who bore it well, who were practiced in accommodating their various obligations, and who were pretty good at striking balances. They stayed on the middle-of-the-course road. They compromised, and their compromises, if not elegant, were workable: their originally inconsistent attitude about schoolhouse religion symbolized this messy process of practical adjustment. They played things by ear, trying to avoid bitterness, to escape setting off a trigger-happy community, and to keep the people from becoming emotional.

They saw the pros and cons, as Murphy pointed out. They were moderates in temperament, conciliators in behavior, and optimistic in outlook, working hard "to get their feelings under control" and to help "the people . . . adjust themselves" to change. "Any change brings a certain amount of insecurity," said Rynne solicitously; but each of the five was aware of the fact that time usually healed wounds and that "usage brings about a lot of things."

The liberateds were unquestionably committed to the task of making their feelings consonant with the Court's ethic on prayers. The Court had given them a focal point to converge on, clear and unequivocal. The clarity of the Court and the school board was a good thing. There was no other course, no alternative but to obey—but these were not nulist assertions of the Court's omnipotence and punitiveness. These limits were conscientious limitations, arising from a duty to respond to a citizen's code. Perhaps each of the five would have moved more quickly to the Court's attitudes if the matter had affected only himself. Where matters affected others, however, gradualism was more important than swiftness. They responded to the focal point as best they could, given the complexity of their other loyalties. They needed time to search for ways to meet apparently incompatible but irrevocable obligations. In no sense did they permanently commit themselves to straddle the fence; they knew the side of the fence where they had finally to come to rest, but they were obliged to help their communities (their staff, their parents, their children) get over the fence, too, without pulling them apart, without public upheaval, without rending them asunder. They wanted to get on with the tasks at hand, but they knew that unless the people were content the tasks could not be done.

What was striking about these liberateds was their sensitivity to the reactions of their community. Their door was open; their ears were to the ground. They were concerned about the community's tolerance of changes. Did the teachers, or the parents, or even the students, draw the wrong inferences? Had the decision maker taken precautions to control social expectations? Farley, in the first interview, was asked, "Would you like or dislike the practice of daily Bible reading in morning assembly?" He responded: "No, I don't do it here. But I would continue the Bible reading if my predecessor had started it. I wouldn't want them to feel I was against the Bible." If the people were quiet, if they were not getting the wrong impression, then changes could be stepped up. If they were edgy, more gradual change was appropriate. They had great respect for men who could handle the introduction of change without upsetting the citizenry.

One of the liberateds resembled a backlasher. Farley proudly boasted of the Christmas play his elementary school performed after the prayer ban. But in fact Farley was not like Mareno or Cagney personally writing a little skit, purposefully violating the spirit of the prayer ban. At the second interview he no longer had strong cognitions about the essentiality of religion to character development. Between interviews he had watered down the strength of the relationship between the two to the point where "I've got to admit that it [schoolhouse religion] has been worthless, if I say so." His observation was no different from Murphy's belief that "the schools aren't too important" in the religious development of the child; from Miss Mercer's assertion that the prayer ban had really had no consequences; from Miss Barrone's hesitant conjecture about religion's impact on morals, "We might think these things are so, but how do we know?"

Farley was no militant and bitter man. Consider his reaction to the prayer ban. At the outset he tried to whip up public interest; he formed a committee for retention of school prayer, drummed up publicity, circulated petitions, and spent his time coordinating all these efforts. He got disappointingly little effective support for his pains, from which he concluded, "The population of Midland . . . felt that their kids were getting enough indoctrination at home and at the church, and it wasn't too important at school." Not finding the people discontent, assured that none of his constituents regarded him as non-religious, he nearly forgot his concern for prayers as he searched about for some other cause to undertake on behalf of the people against "the boys downtown."

Farley had every reason to feel negative about his job, the school system, the Supreme Court, and the prayer cases. He was in work he found restricting; he had just been publicly rebuked by the school board for his inept administration of his elementary school; the Court had condemned a traditional service he had been extending the parents of his community for years. But if he was bleeding, he was bleeding inwardly, and he still retained pride in the good he was doing his community; he was a Don Quixote, but one with considerable self-esteem.

The liberateds were sanguine people, reposing trust in the polity, in the Supreme Court, even in the school board. They were willing to give the Court the benefit of the doubt. It was as if they each said that from the Court's vantage point, who knows but maybe the problem has dimensions unseen from the parochial perspectives of Midland public schools. Murphy remarked that the Catholic Justice Brennan agreed with the decision. Miss Mercer explained the quiet reaction of her community as a function of the fact that the people came to understand the opinion, as if to say that she never questioned its correctness but was only worried that the parents and the school children might draw the wrong inferences from it. Miss Barrone noted of the justices, "After all, their decisions have been pretty good, you know, and we have to have some faith in the Supreme Court."

This deference to the Court by virtue of its larger perspectives was striking. It was trusting, not suspicious; national, not insular; cooperative, not alien; responsive, not reactionary. The Court was delegated the job of settling disagreements on which reasonable men took different sides; its decisions were binding, and the liberateds' responsibility was to bridge, not straddle, the gap between the people and the Court.

The liberateds were, to use Dahl's term, political professionals,[8] little leaders who had committed themselves wholeheartedly to the Midland organization, who had served for years variously and widely and hence

[8] Robert A. Dahl, *Who Governs?* (New Haven: Yale University Press, 1961), pp. 305-10.

had status and authority throughout the system. For example, Rynne was cited by Miss Barber as a man of courage. As for Farley, at least four principals, enemies and friends alike, mentioned him in some connection (no other principal was cited by his colleagues more than once.)

In the microcosms of their neighborhoods, these little professionals looked to the bigger professionals to see how to handle dilemmas. Take Murphy, the senior high school principal, for instance. He was a tough, emphatic Irishman, tight-lipped and sentimental to the quick. As president of the teachers' association for six years, he had bargained with Mayor Fiorito successfully for sizeable increases in teachers' salaries and had developed such admiration for the mayor that his eyes filmed over with feeling whenever he mentioned Fiorito's name.

What was the example Fiorito set for Murphy? It was the mayor's suggestion of silent meditation that earned Murphy's admiration, and the lesson of the suggestion was that a leader must search out and accommodate the psychological needs of his people if they had needs, must fill the void if a void was created.

Little leaders taking their cues from big ones, the liberateds set forth to complete the doing of the gigantic job the Court could only initiate but never complete without cooperation—the task of fitting the Court's lessons into the hearts of the people.

The sources of this political sense of the little professionals are very obscure. For Miss Barrone, it may have been her father, bringing home his cronies to talk about the politics of the old country and the new, who trained her "to take the interpretation of the people we admire and who will lead us." For Miss Mercer, it may have been her uncle, who sat as the first president of Midland's town council. It may just have been the liberateds' universal social delight in joining groups, with its consequences of multiple cross-obligations, which gave them empathy for the moral conflicts of their fellow man. Self-sufficient, unindignant, trying to understand the prayer decision, not to berate it, they knuckled down like pros to the task of closing the ranks, of keeping education out of the political realm, of preserving the system from cranks and know-nothings. Liberated from their uncertainty of purpose by the big leaders' deference to the Supreme Court, they had their feelings under control and into some tolerable consistency by the time of the second interview. In another year, perhaps, the wounds would have all healed and the scars would be hardly perceptible.

Reverse Liberateds

Rizzuto, Miss O'Hara, and Miss Kennedy became favorable toward schoolhouse religion, whereas they had originally been, at least equivocally, critical.

In the first interviews the reverse liberateds were notable because they urged an elimination policy. Of the 17 Catholics in the sample, only these three were in agreement with the about-to-be-announced rule of the Court. They were deviates from the Catholic norm in Midland in their desire to deemphasize religious practices in the public schoolroom.

Their position was maintained with considerable misgiving. Their extreme position meant social discomfort for them. Furthermore, commitment to deemphasizing religious practices in the school did not entirely fit their optimistic outlooks. For example, the sanguine Rizzuto, with his views of a trend toward religious tolerance among the younger generation, had genuine difficulty in squaring his commitment to deemphasis with the scanty necessity for it.

But worst of all consequences was the implication of their commitment to deemphasis for their religious self-respect. Each was devout, yet each found himself having to bolster his deviate position on schoolhouse religion against the attacks of his devout friends. One way of doing so was to derogate his own Catholic Church. Inevitably, because the priests argued for a more unionist position, these three reverse liberateds began to oppose (at least in their minds) the priests.

Unquestionably, the increasingly visible gap between the consensus of Catholic congregants and the reverse liberateds, visible to no one more than to the reverse liberateds themselves, was extremely unsettling. They began to see their commitment to deemphasis as an irreligious act, and their doubts were hardly assuaged when their acquaintances implied that there was something godless about the three of them. They felt they were failing to give support to the Church. Their commitment to deemphasis of prayer at that time somehow was inconsistent with their self-concepts of how religious they were.[9]

[9] Cf., *Brehm and Cohen,* p. 59: "Consider, for example, a person who believes himself highly religious but who fails on a given holy day to attend or support a church. The cognition about his behavior could be quite undeniable and explicit in signifying irreligiousness. Yet we would expect him to have prior commitment to his self-concept about how religious a

This doubt about their religiousness was hard to deny, because all three of these reverse liberateds were alike in their vivacity and gregarious propensities. Three extraordinarily energetic personalities, all loved to talk, to think aloud, to join debate. These three were professionals, too, active socially (Rizzuto and Miss O'Hara scaled at the top of the school board and the staff respectively on the Social Activities Index) and with status among the system's personnel. Yet every contact, unless it steered clear of the religious issue, brought the threat of conflict.

Their commitments to deemphasizing schoolhouse religion came from different sources. For Miss O'Hara and Miss Kennedy, they came from the experience of administering public schools in Jewish neighborhoods. Each had experienced trouble with Jewish parents objecting to patently sectarian practices.

Rizzuto's commitment was the result of Goldman's effort on the school board. By the first interview Goldman had already informed the school board of the implications of the New York Regents' prayer case, and Rizzuto had had time to adapt his feelings to the position Goldman told him the Court was going to take.

The liberating hypothesis would predict that the reverse liberateds would react in a non-obvious way to the prayer ban. We would expect that their earlier commitment to deemphasis had aroused considerable personal concern which in turn was motivating all three to adapt their feelings before *Schempp*. At the same time, the attitude adjustments presumably impugned their religious self-respect. Each, therefore, I would predict, must eventually try to rebuild his religious self-image. The Supreme Court decision and the school board's prayer ban would solve the dilemma of the two conflicting tendencies: the one of building up critical attitudes toward schoolhouse religion, and the other of reestablishing religiousness. The *Schempp* ruling, I would predict, would take the heat off the three to maintain their commitment to religious deemphasis since it had been accomplished.

Furthermore, by developing attitudes slightly discrepant from the

---

man he was. Hence, he would be expected to experience dissonance by building up the relevant parts of his self-concept. We would, in short, look for this person to increase the strength of his belief that he was highly religious. There is, of course, a limit to this kind of distortion. Nevertheless, this is an additional way in which negative reactions or boomerangs can occur from the arousal of dissonance."

scapegoat Supreme Court, they would establish with their friends a political image distinct from the justices. Thereby, they could indicate their religiousness and their desire to remain a part of their social circles.

In fact, this process of reconciliation was exactly what happened. The reverse liberateds lapsed back from their originally deviate commitment. In renouncing her previous position of deemphasis, Miss O'Hara even went so far as to express a liking for the conduct of church school classes by clergymen in public school buildings.

One factor in bringing about this regression was the assassination of President Kennedy (Miss Kennedy said of it: "I guess I thought to myself: 'Isn't it a shame that we couldn't resort to a prayer of some sort?' "). The death of a beloved president and coreligionist—this incongruous, unexpected, fateful event—suddenly seemed to "expose themselves to themselves."[10] It was as if the reverse liberateds suddenly caught themselves peeking at their own sacrilege. Their anxiety over their irreligiousness spilled over to such a point that they had to uncommit themselves from their previous elimination stance.

In these reverse liberateds, then, there was evidence of a negative reaction to the Court decision, yet this boomerang effect was more apparent than real. Each ended up with mild patriot self-images, comparable to the liberateds'. There was little anxiety about the omission of prayer from the school curriculum insofar as character development was concerned. The intensity of their feelings was greatly diminished. For example, Rizzuto had originally described those citizens who wished to eradicate religion from school as "inverse bigots or hypersensitive communicants"; in the second interview he saw the opponents of prayer as persons "who do not concur . . . and have a right not to have this belief imposed on them when they don't want it." And finally, for at least two—Rizzuto and Miss O'Hara—their feelings about the Supreme Court reversed: where they had felt unfavorably toward it, they developed a modest respect for it.

Their reaction was not against the Court but against their self-doubts about how religious they were. The Court decision simply removed the motivation to be in the forefront of the movement toward deemphasis. With the prayer ban in force, they could reestablish their solidarity with all the other professionals in the system. Their reaction looked militant when it was merely reminiscent. They were paying

[10] Helen Merrill Lynd, *On Shame and the Search for Identity* (New York: Harcourt, Brace, 1958), pp. 27-43.

their respects to a feeling they had helped to kill. They would slowly put it out of mind with the return of their religious self-respect.

The Vindicated

Derzon, Goldman, Mrs. Hanna, Leonard, Miss Cohen, Kaplan, and Woodford remained critical of schoolhouse religion.

None of the vindicated was Catholic in religion or conservative in their domestic politics. Four were Jewish, and three Protestant; all but two practiced their faith formally. Six were liberal—all but Miss Cohen. All but two—Kaplan and Miss Cohen—were favorably predisposed to the Supreme Court in the original interview. Only two—Kaplan and Miss Cohen—scored above zero on the Social Activities Index, and they scaled a modest two.

Inasmuch as the Court decision was in line with their original predispositions on the subject of prayers, cognitive dissonance theory would predict that the vindicated would be less motivated than before the *Schempp* case to listen closely to supporting information. Compared to the backlashers, the converts, and the liberateds, whose original viewpoints were contrary to the Court's rule, the theory would predict for the vindicated a much diminished search for credible and reliable sources to support their commitments to deemphasis.[11]

For Mrs. Hanna and Leonard, such was the case. While Leonard had read the Court's decision, Mrs. Hanna had not; both, however, had delegated the matters of prayers to Goldman and had turned to more immediate concerns: the curriculum and classroom pedagogy. Two of the most thoroughgoing persons in the sample, neither paid attention to the supportive opinions of officials in nearby states. Neither gave much attention to the supportive opinion of their own state attorney general. So far as Mrs. Hanna and Leonard were concerned, the subject was closed when the Court ruled.

The remaining five, however, did not diminish their attention to supportive materials. The Court's decision and the school board's ban, consonant as they were with their original commitments, sharpened the social conflict around them. Even though they were relatively remote from the system's social affairs, all four Jews and the Negro Woodford

[11] Cf., J. S. Adams, "Reduction of Cognitive Dissonance by Seeking Consonant Information," *Journal of Abnormal Social Psychology,* 62 (1961), 74-78: "A person in whom dissonance has been produced by exposure to an *authoritative* communication espousing a contrary point of view on an *important subject* is more likely to seek authoritative information on the subject than a person who has been exposed to a consonant communication."

began to experience heightened anti-Semitic and anti-Negro feelings among the system's Catholic members. The Court's opinion increased the social hostility against their previously innocuous separatism. Kaplan experienced perhaps the most direct attack, but it was clear that widespread social bitterness occurred as a result of the ban. Woodford, a devout Episcopalian, was concerned about anti-Negro backlash because the prayer ban was identified with the predominantly Negro Jehovah's Witnesses and the Black Muslims.

These four Jews and one Negro, more attentively than before the Court's opinion in *Schempp,* searched for authoritative sources to confirm their separatist views. Unquestionably the most important communication was the opinion of the state attorney general, a well-known and respected Catholic and a Midland native. While the opinion served as ammunition to refute the vocal Catholic criticism, its most important use to the vindicateds was its reassurance that the prayer ban would eventually be accepted by Catholics and that a feud could be avoided between Catholics on the one hand and Negroes and Jews on the other. The attorney general's opinion confirmed their hopes that the system would be preserved.

Cognitive dissonance theory would also predict that the prayer ban, by eliminating the discrepancy between the vindicateds' commitment to deemphasis and the earlier devotional policies within the system, would reduce the need for bolstering their separatist attitudes with exclusively confirmatory evidence. To put it another way, they would be more receptive to opposed views—they would be more open-minded.

This tolerance of opposed views did occur. By the time of the second interview, five of the seven indicated a tolerance of more religious practice in the schoolroom than they had before *Schempp,* and the undertone of anger which used to underlie the vindicateds' opinion about the proponents of schoolhouse religion ceased. Insight replaced indignation. The eloquent Mrs. Hanna put their newly developed and unmoralized judgments of their opposition this way:

I think those who architect formal learning have to pay attention to the development of the inner man. We can't avoid this. The wonderful thing about organized religion is that it asks a wonderful series of questions—even though they proceed to give a lot of perfectly silly answers. The questions are important, and some procedures should be worked out to indicate to your young people that these are serious and normal questions: man's reaction to nature and to each other, and so forth. Formal education has to do something about this. What people who are so very zealous about prayers really want is this: We wish school people would show young people that these questions are important and that there are adult approaches to them. And they have a point.

This relaxation of the barriers to alien views was not to be confused with temporizing of attitudes. The vindicateds remained separatist, and they remained so with increased confidence in their original estimates of the harm schoolhouse religion inflicted on certain students. But increased certainty did not mean increased militancy. Rather, the vindicateds wanted to mend fences, to keep the system together. Kaplan introduced silent meditation. Woodford continued the recital of P.T.A. prayers at P.T.A. meetings. Woodford, Leonard, and Goldman wanted to institute courses in comparative religion where before they had opposed them. All seven—with the possible exception of Kaplan—supported the lay staff plan for moral enrichment of the curriculum. The vindicateds put their insight to work by assuaging the worries of their former opponents and by giving assurances that there would be no abuses of the legal advantage the Court had given them.

All seven felt some obligation to the Supreme Court. The *Schempp* opinion not only vindicated their judgments. They looked to the decision for suggestions of how to mitigate the non-separatists' doubts about the implications of the decision. The part of the decision which the vindicateds remembered was the language of concession. When the Court suggested the usefulness of comparative religion courses, the vindicateds took up the cudgels in behalf of this idea as a means of reconciliation. The converts, the liberateds, the nulists, even the backlashers were less motivated to look at the safety valves in the Court decision than were the vindicateds.

Perhaps one way of looking at the change is that the legal decision of *Schempp* shifted the personal responsibility for the administration of character building in the school system from the unionists to the separatists. In shifting the worry about maintaining the organization, the legal decision imposed sharp and immediate constraints upon the behavior of the legal victors, and the language of restraint used by the Court was entirely consonant with their new responsibilities. The aggressiveness, the militancy, the bitterness, and the stridency of their original views gave way to concern about preserving the vested interest of all the educators in the school system.

VII

The Force of Law

The remarkable fact was that none of the twenty-eight public school officials simply ignored or distorted the *Schempp* decision. Why did they pay attention to the law? And why did they ultimately hear the message so accurately?

Salience of the Law

If salience means unforgettability, the prayer cases and the board's prayer ban were salient to the twenty-eight public school officials. Twenty-two of them were able to call to mind some important aspect of the *Schempp* case, and all twenty-eight knew exactly what exercises the ban prohibited in Midland public schools.

Even more revealing as to just how unforgettable law can be were the results of the original interview. The Supreme Court decided *Engel v. Vitale* some seven months before the original interviews; in that case the New York State Regents' Prayer was declared unconstitutional, and the decision had immediate salience for all twenty-eight respondents. In response to two questions—what and why did the Court decide in *Engel*—twenty-one of them mentioned accurately at least one of five factual or legal details: a state agency composed the prayer; provision was made to excuse non-believing children from its recital; the decision depended on an interpretation of the Fourteenth Amendment of the United States Constitution; the Establishment Clause of the First Amendment was involved indirectly through its incorporation in the Fourteenth Amendment; and the Establishment Clause was colloquially known as the doctrine of separation of church and state. Even those who found it highly annoying kept it in their consciousness, apparently giving it a great deal of thought in the seven months intervening between the Court decision and the original interview.

In contrast, none of the private school headmasters accurately mentioned one of these five details in response to the same two questions. These five persons never thought the *Engel* case pertinent. It was an event, noticed in the papers, perhaps inquired about briefly, but then buried out of mind by news of greater consequence. "Inevitably," apologized one headmaster, "human nature thinks about what affects it; and this decision does not affect us."

The law relating to schoolhouse religion obviously encroached upon the public school administrator's consciousness a year before *Schempp.* Why was it so salient? Because the law was justiciable; because those public school officials somehow knew that judges in courtrooms would apply it if the matter was brought to their attention; because law spelled trouble.

The observant Dr. Johnson, Boswell tells us, once remarked, "Law supplies the weak with adventitious strength."[1] Dahl, a contemporary political scientist, made the same point in his study of *Who Governs?*: "One set of officials—judges—can . . . confer [the mantle of legality] on the actions of private citizens."[2] And the fretful pediatrician Dr. Clancy more colloquially, but with no less force, asserted the identical thought:

> It's like the cops who put a no-parking sign out. I don't like it, but the police department is the authoritative body. She may be only Mrs. Jones across the street. She hasn't got anything done, she's ineffectual, but she can insist on my upholding the law. She calls in and suddenly has tremendous power.

Law is salient because it gives the right to judicial review, not just to political elites or to religious leaders or to educators, who might be counted on to use moderation or discretion, but to private citizens, who are unpredictable and vindictive, who, as Miss O'Hara put it, do not always realize what they are doing. The individual "Mrs. Jones across the street" can haul the highest official before a judge in a

[1] James Boswell, *Life of Johnson* (London: Oxford University Press, 1953), reprinted in *The World of Law* (ed., Ephraim London), Vol. II, p. 76 (New York: Simon and Schuster, 1960).

[2] Robert A. Dahl, *Who Governs?* (New Haven: Yale University Press, 1961), p. 247.

public courtroom. Since the judge is not going to ignore the law in deciding what to do about the matter, it does the individual administrator little good to be legally ignorant. To know the law is not necessarily to follow it, but awareness at least gives a freedom of choice between obedience and a self-destructive collision with the adventitious strength of Mrs. Jones.

Favorable Interpretation of the Law

If *Schempp* was undeniable, one possible remaining response was making it inapplicable, to interpret it in the most wishful light and thereby to lessen the discrepancy between it and one's personal attitudes. The risk to one's self-image as a law-abiding citizen is lessened; besides, it might be possible to bluff Mrs. Jones out of invoking the law by acknowledging that the law exists and then claiming to be within it.

Wishful interpretation occurred in connection with *Engel* but not with *Schempp,* although the wording of the opinions provided similar opportunities to distort the legal message—if individual officials wanted to. Not only was it possible to read *Schempp* so narrowly as to permit the Midland practice; State Commissioner Foley and the school boards of Northland and Milltown officially approved of just such a narrow interpretation of it.

Fifteen of the seventeen professional educators who were originally non-separatist, were nonetheless sure that the Court had meant the broad (and unfavorable from their point of view) construction of its opinion: to eliminate all devotional exercises from public schools. In the sense that 88 per cent took no benefit of the doubt, there was no distortion of the legal message despite the opportunity for it.

If we are to believe the evidence, the activity of the lawyer Goldman prevented the officials from giving a narrow and favorable interpretation. Twenty-six of the twenty-seven officials mentioned his crucial role. The prayer ban was invariably referred to as Goldman's proposal. Professor Hanna put it most eloquently: he "assume[d] command and precipitate[d] decision by clarifying our thinking."

Goldman, the son of a New York lawyer, came to Midland after law school to clerk for a federal judge, who (in Goldman's words) "worked harder at being a judge—God, he cared! He wouldn't be satisfied until his intellectual, emotional and ethical feelings came into some kind of coincidence." After his clerkship, Goldman stayed in Midland to open his private practice, and, as his father had, he devoted considerable time to the problems of civil rights. For example, he had played a part in the Jewish group's demand to deemphasize Christian observances in Northland, which had so badly sundered the suburb in 1961. He was a loyal Democrat, devoted to Mayor Fiorito, and when the mayor decided that the school board ought to have someone on it to give free and timely legal advice, Goldman was the obvious choice.

Goldman was devoted to the Supreme Court of the United States. Indeed, he was identified with it so completely that it seemed inseparable from him.[3] When asked how he personally felt on eight major issues, each of which had been dealt with by the Court, his personal choice and the judicial outcome exactly coincided. There was no indecision on his part, even though each of the issues was sufficiently complicated to cause the twenty-seven other respondents considerable difficulty.

Goldman was not a blind follower of the Court's decisions. He was a critic of their details and of the justices' craftsmanship. It happened, however, that his moral and intellectual inclinations were the same as the justices'. Years earlier he had learned and integrated their major premises into his personality. When a social problem arose, the justices in Washington and the lawyer in Midland searched for the presence of the same critical factors, related them to the same values, ascertained the same causes, and arrived—not surprisingly—at the same remedies. To use Miss Barrone's word, it would have "shocked" Goldman if his personal decision and the Court's opinion had not coincided.

Furthermore, as a student of the Supreme Court, he saw its role (and hence his) very distinctly. Its job in the political process was to decide difficult problems, not the really important social issues that could be illuminated by public debate and democratic procedures—taxes, the domestic welfare, or foreign affairs—but the counter-productive ones that paralyzed and broke down the democratic processes. Translated into the Midland context, his view meant that, as the Court's local representative, he had to divert the reflex of public opinion to the prayer decision from the mayor and the rest of the school board onto himself. He did so by personally shouldering the

[3] "A person identifies himself with a group when, in making a decision, he evaluates the several alternatives of choice in terms of their consequences for the specified group." Herbert A. Simon, *Administrative Behavior* (New York: Macmillan, 1947), p. 205. See Herbert Kaufman, *The Forest Ranger* (Baltimore: Johns Hopkins University Press, 1960), pp. 175 ff., for a stimulating discussion of the building of identification.

responsibility for listening for the legal message, translating it into local terms without distortion, and focusing the people's attention on the source of that message: the Supreme Court of the United States. He was, in cybernetic terms, the community receptor; he was "at the decisive middle level of communication and decision."[4]

Goldman obtained clarity in Midland by patience, self-sacrifice, and threat. He was gradual with the school board; he acted as a scapegoat for the educational staff; and he blackmailed the Midland political elite.

Gradualism on the School Board

Goldman introduced the school board and the two superintendents to the problem of public school prayer exactly six months before *Schempp* was decided and almost nine months before the board had to publish its prayer ban. At the time he submitted his confidential memorandum on the implications of *Engel,* five of the nine board members and superintendents held strong non-separatist attitudes, while four (including Goldman) were separatist.

Goldman stimulated discussion at a time when there was no urgent need for a policy change. The matter was academic, detached from real consequences. The public was not aware of what the board talked about—no law suits were in the offing, and the staff was quiet. Goldman, however, could demand that the board devote some attention to his subject, because, as the legal specialist of the board, he was expected to anticipate legal developments, however remote. Discussion time was conventionally allotted to whatever subjects he detected as potentially troublesome. This earlier discussion laid the groundwork for the law's impact on attitudes.

In this seminar-like atmosphere, the seven board members (later they were joined by the two superintendents) began their personal reflections on the ticklish subject of schoolhouse religion. Each expressed his personal feelings, not so much to oppose his colleagues' attitudes, but to clarify the others' expectations of him. Goldman expressed his reservations about devotionals in the public schools but took time to disabuse Rizzuto of the idea that he was hostile to religion. Clancy, in his hesitant, sincere way, had a chance to put into words how important his religious education had been to him. This leisurely talk was vital, for, after all, while they had worked long hours together on a variety of projects, they had never talked about their religious beliefs

[4] Karl W. Deutsch, *The Nerves of Government* (New York: Free Press of Glencoe, 1963), p. 154.

and practices. They had to feel each other out in this new area, assuring themselves none would scorn deep emotions. In short, this group of adults had to develop trust by first expressing in measured steps their areas of agreement. Only then was the airing of differences possible.

The development of mutual trust permitted the breaking down of the formal barriers between them. In turn, informality allowed free, less defensive discussion of new ideas (such as the possibility that the Court might declare recital of all prayer unconstitutional and the suitability of silent prayer in its place). New concepts such as pluralism and separatism could be contributed to conversation impersonally, as suggestions, not commands, allowing each member voluntarily to try fitting them into his own frame of reference.[5]

The first accomplishment of this fitting process was agreement that while the board had choice to comply with or ignore a Court decision, they would choose to obey the law, whatever it was, out of their responsibility as leaders. Goldman thus established the element of volition and obtained a commitment of compliance.

The second achievement was that the participants in the conversation made, and were urged to make, distinctions. The vague concept of prayers was defined and redefined intellectually, consecutively shearing off satellite connotations. Clancy, for example, began to distinguish prayer recitals from "our teaching . . . some sense of wonder." By separating philosophy from prayer, he preserved philosophy in the schools and thereby diminished the importance of prayer. Similar intellectual distinctions as to religiousness, individual guidance, ethics, and moral development further deflated the emotional values involved in public school prayers.

For those whose educational philosophies were predicated on their religious beliefs, such distinctions in turn required modifications in their ideas of what schools were for and how character developed in a secular culture. Goldman gave time to the board to adapt these inter-

[5] The informality and subtlety of Goldman's leadership on this matter during the months before *Schempp* can be inferred from the original interviews. In the original interviews, none of the six board members (excluding Goldman) except Leonard mentioned the Goldman memorandum, and Leonard could not "remember what the conclusion was." Yet none of the six thought non-compliance with the Court would be permissible. Only two members thought any form of prayer in the classrooms would be constitutional (in contrast to 79 per cent of the principals). Five of the six mentioned silent prayer as a possible compromise (in contrast to 26 per cent of the principals).

related attitudes in anticipation of the *Schempp* decision. When old attitudes undergo modification and previously emotional concepts are rendered less passionate, serious self-doubt can, and did, arise. "There was a lot of soul searching," Dr. Bartkowicz said with a sigh. Those who were in the midst of changing their original opinions kept seeing themselves as traitors to their religious and social communities. They feared that the entire tissue of their beliefs was critically weakened by the excision of long-held premises.

The job of fitting the new attitudes into the place of the old was custom work, which could not be done on a mass basis and a quick reading of the Supreme Court opinion. Nor could it be done by the compassionate Goldman, whose particular skeptical and intellectual inheritance was so alien to the devout frame of reference which some of his colleagues shared. The special fitting had to be done by the devout individual himself. (Miss O'Hara said: "I had to do my own reconciling of the decision we were making with my own dogma.")

This slow, self-teaching process permitted most of the board members to get rid of their indecision in privacy. By the time they had to bear public scrutiny, they had self-respect, intellectual coordination, and certitude.

The Community's Scapegoat

Although the school board and the superintendents were prepared for the decision gradually, the remainder of the Midland educational organization was not. The principals, the classroom staff, and the interested public were not refitting their attitudes in anticipation of *Schempp*. The evidence in regard to the principals indicates they were initially lulled into a wishful optimism by a number of events, chiefly the statements of Commissioner Foley. The prayer ban of the school board was therefore a shock.

More importantly, it was an accusation of wrongdoing ("Many teachers took it as if they had done wrong all these years, and they knew they hadn't," said Miss Barrone). In a small disciplined group like the school board, it was possible to talk these feelings out in confidence, to make distinctions and to avoid feelings of wrongdoing before the ban was issued. In the case of the principals, however, neither time nor informal groups were available to Goldman to moderate the staff's reactions before the ban was imposed.

Goldman and the school board members were aware of their limitations in these respects. In the original interview, Mrs. Hanna was asked if she would like the school board to initiate a limitation on school prayers. Her reply was "No—we could not get it accepted." The board alone had no means to disabuse the staff of the idea that the prayer ban was a personal denunciation. The consequences of a board-initiated prayer ban would be the arousal of anxiety and hostility against the school board and a breakdown of organization morale.

Mrs. Hanna then correctly asserted that the prayer ban "is most likely to be accepted if the Supreme Court makes it." What differences did a Court decision make?

The ancients were said occasionally to place upon a goat's head the symbols of the sins of the people and afterward to permit the goat to escape into the wilderness. In this way the guilt feelings were discharged at the expense of the non-offending animal, and expiation was achieved by the community. The Supreme Court and its local representative—Goldman—resembled scapegoats.[6] The Midland staff became angry at the prayer ban, but not at the school board or themselves. It took its aggression out on the Supreme Court and of course on Goldman.

If we are to believe Woodford and Kaplan, the majority of the principals bitterly denounced Goldman after his talk to them, and his Jewishness was more often than not a focus for a personal attack. But by putting the blame on him, they never had to attribute anti-religious attitudes to the rest of Midland officialdom: Mayor Fiorito, Dr. Bartkowicz, even the rest of the school board. In fact, the episode may have increased their feelings of solidarity with the system.

The blameworthy Goldman, like the goat who retreated to the wilderness, also had his escape—in his profession, his personality, and his predilections. He was not vulnerable to the face-to-face rebuke received by the political leaders out front, like Chairman Rizzuto and Dr. Clancy. These susceptible men were free to divert the community hostility onto the Court and Goldman. But while Goldman could escape the force of the personal denunciation, his reputation was severely damaged. To the extent his prestige waned, his influence in later situations was diminished. His own self-perceptions, however, demanded such personal sacrifice. As he saw it, he and the Court, by

[6] David Riesman, *Individualism Reconsidered* (Glencoe: Free Press, 1954), pp. 440-466, 450. Cf. Jack Peltason, *58 Lonely Men* (New York: Harcourt, Brace, 1961), a description of the economic, social, and psychological retaliation inflicted on Southern federal judges responsible for imposing desegregation in the South.

acting as scapegoats, could protect the board from attack so that it could solve "some really relatively sticky matters": racial imbalance, curriculum and disciplinary reform. In these important matters community support would have to be mobilized, and that job necessarily would fall to the political leaders like Chairman Rizzuto, Dr. Bartkowicz, Mayor Fiorito, even perhaps Dr. Clancy.

The Loan of Political Resources

Dr. Clancy, a member of the Midland political elite more by virtue of his marriage than by his experience, once asked: "Do the people have to adhere to what the Supreme Court decides? What happens if they don't comply?" The answer to his first question is "under some circumstances, no"; to the second, "it depends." What happens to the leaders of the people—the political officials—if they refuse to obey judges? What powers have the judges?

Men have suggested many sources of judicial power. Charles Evans Hughes attributed the Supreme Court's influence to its "intellectual power conscientiously applied."[7] We have seen the affection for the Court felt by some Midland officials, particularly Negroes, for past decisions; undoubtedly these feelings gave the Court a measure of influence. Perhaps other political assets which the Supreme Court has could be added if I sought to catalogue them.

But unquestionably there are times when the Court's own resources are insufficient to obtain local compliance. One such time in Midland was approximately six weeks before election day, 1963, when community feeling against the prayer ban was at its height and at its most unpredictable. If Miss O'Hara's version of the story is accurate, it was then that "Mayor Fiorito at last . . . decided he would have to rescind the board's policy: the pressures were terrific." Her story was corroborated by Goldman and Leonard. The Supreme Court was not in a position where it could offset the losses Mayor Fiorito would personally incur by obeying the Court. Defeat in the forthcoming election meant more than losing a steady paycheck and a future political career. In Mayor Fiorito's case, these personal losses were relatively inconsiderable. A loss, however, meant the crushing of his public aspirations for Midland: the cessation of efforts to eradicate urban blight, racial segregation, and stubborn ignorance. The Court could do nothing to compensate the risk of a personal defeat or diminish the electoral

[7] Charles Evans Hughes, *The Supreme Court of the United States* (Garden City: Garden City, 1936), p. 57.

uncertainties which the prayer ban seemed (to Fiorito) to introduce into the campaign. Only persons in the Midland community could affect Fiorito's assessment of the local situation. One such man was Goldman.

Why did Goldman have any resources at all? The answer lay in his earlier service to the community. He had established credit for those gratuitous contributions with a wide number of fellow citizens. He had subtly explained away—to the public's satisfaction—an inept statement by Dr. Bartkowicz about a matter related to curriculum, thereby saving the superintendent acute embarrassment. He had successfully mediated labor disputes for the city. He had given eloquent and timely support to administration proposals. He had given countless hours to countless causes. And of course he had met the prayer cases decisively. As a result, on the school board alone there were three colleagues willing to resign if Goldman gave the signal.

Goldman called on this credit to blackmail Mayor Fiorito into compliance. When Fiorito was about to rescind the board's ban, Goldman confronted him with his own resignation and with the threatened resignations of others and with demoralization of the mayor's most dedicated followers. Political danger is a relative matter, and the defection of Goldman appeared to the mayor a disaster greater than the danger which the Court's prayer case presented.

"Do the people have to adhere to what the Supreme Court decides?" The answer is yes when local adherents of the Supreme Court put their political influence on the line to make non-adherence more costly than compliance to the Court.[8]

Legal Colleagues

Few Midland lawyers shared Goldman's wholehearted identification with the Supreme Court. Some members of the legal fraternity sought to distort the Court's message: Rizzuto's acquaintances were more interested in evading the decision than conforming to it; the lawyers Dr. Clancy knew denounced the board for not exploiting the loopholes in

[8] Cf. Aaron Wildavsky, *Dixon-Yates* (New Haven: Yale University Press, 1962), p. 321: "One part of the job of forging a coalition based on a broadly appealing objective is to enhance its desirability by doing things to make alternatives look worse. 'Desirability' is a relative concept. A person's evaluation of his experience may be favorable or unfavorable depending on his basis for comparison."

Schempp; Miss Barber's brother-in-law sent her a denunciation of the Court; Woodford's legal friend thought it was a bad decision.

At the same time Goldman was not alone in toiling in the Court's behalf. Jim Holden advised the teachers' association to comply; the city corporation counsel told the mayor to accept the prayer ban; the state attorney general rebuked Commissioner Foley; one Republican lawyer divided his party on the prayer issue by supporting the Democratic mayor's school board at the height of the campaign. When Goldman was denounced for his stand, these four colleagues, all lawyers in the limelight, rallied to his aid and repeated the Court's message to those who wished not to hear it. It was not much company, but it was enough to be reassuring, and their prestige gave an appearance of unanimity in the Midland legal profession.

VIII

Summary

Over and over again in the interviews the officials described the personal impact of the prayer cases in physical terms. The law touched a "sore point"; it made a "wound"; it took a "slice out of our thunder"; it left a "scar." To these men and women the change in attitude which they had undergone was like a medical operation in which the morbid part of an organ is excised.

If I follow through with the surgical metaphor to which the respondents naturally gravitated, it highlights four important circumstances about the process of attitude change. A successful physical operation requires a patient who is willing to undergo its discomforts; it needs surgeons and nurses whom the patient trusts; it calls for the use of sharp and functional instruments to minimize the intrusion; and there must follow a convalescent period in which new tissues can form to bind the incision. Not too dissimilarly, attitude change involves the individual's incentive to excise old attitudes, trustworthy associates who aid the individual to adapt, the intellectual tools to confine psychological repercussions to a minimum, and a social environment sufficiently compatible to permit new attitudes to develop.

The Motive to Change

Most of the twenty-eight men and women we have observed were originally equivocators. To some degree they espoused two or more incompatible attitudes on the same subject at the same time. These inconsistencies stemmed from discreet experiences. They learned in childhood that the Supreme Court was valuable and in adolescence that judges were hypocrites. Their priests told them that religion was the basis of morality; their history teachers described the religious persecutions which sent the Pilgrims to America; and their college professors said that a non-sectarian religious ceremony gave a nice tone to the classroom. In the period before the *Schempp* case the average Midland official hardly thought twice about the inconsistency which existed, for example, between his personal belief in the more religion the better and his preference for a school policy permitting only a hurried recital of a fifty-word prayer.

Until the *Schempp* case few officials had any motive to integrate their attitudes into a consistent pattern. No one rebuked them for being equivocal. In fact, harboring incompatible attitudes allowed them to adjust to incompatible groups of friends.

The law, however, motivated officials all the way down the line to get their indecision under control. They knew that at least a part of their mixed feelings was outside the law and was bound to get them into trouble with those whom the law vindicated. Furthermore, the teachers looked to the principals, the principals to the school board, and so on, for answers of how to keep out of court or what to do if they were hailed before a magistrate. Everyone in the Midland educational system seemed to know that certain organized groups were looking to this decision as an answer to things they had been hoping for.

The threat of the civil law suit was especially convincing to the average Midland educator because the potential complainants appeared to him so bizarre; they were "atheists", "freethinkers", the "little religions", the "ultraliberals", "a bunch of crackpots", the "inverse bigots," and "hypersensitive communicants," "individualists that like to be a little different", people who indulge in "tactics like the Fascists used", "Communists (Khruschev is an atheist)", persons to whom "something bad psychologically has happened." Schelling has pointed out the special bargaining force of men who refuse to be sensible. "If a man knocks at a door and says that he will stab himself on the porch unless given $10, he is more likely to get the $10 if his eyes are bloodshot."[1] Like the drunk too inebriated to know better, the minority groups that looked to the prayer cases as an answer to things they had been hoping for were likely to be too obstinate or too unin-

[1] Thomas C. Schelling, *The Strategy of Conflict* (Cambridge, Mass.: Harvard University Press, 1960), p. 22.

telligent to realize what they were doing when they brought a lawsuit.[2]

The threat made the official's inherited equivocal feelings an issue. He had a choice: either he had to get his feelings into some kind of coincidence himself, or he could look upward to higher officials to give him guidelines. Somewhere, however, "the buck has to stop", as Mareno put it. A decision had to be made to deal with the imminent threat.

To illustrate the intensity of the pressure upon officials to resolve their indecisiveness, let us look at the fate of State Commissioner Foley. He was a popular man before the *Schempp* case. The former president of Midland's Teachers' College, he was respected by most of the staff in the Midland public school system.

The day *Schempp* was decided, Rynne telephoned him. Miss Barber wrote him. The school board waited expectantly to see what he would do. Other school boards explicitly asked his advice.

Foley did not want to spare time for a decision which he rightly regarded as counterproductive. Miss O'Brien, in her remote little way, was accurate when she said, "The way I see it, he was not excited by it." And so, to Rynne on the phone, "he wouldn't give a definite yes or no." In reply to Miss Barber, "his letters weren't too strong." To Chairman Rizzuto waiting for some guide, "He just didn't make any sense; he said nothing at all about it; it was a lot of doubletalk and worse."

Foley did not resolve his mixed feelings when everyone demanded that he (in Mareno's words) "develop some arguments pro or con the decision or come up with some compromise." Foley did not want to do his homework and to undergo the discomforts of making a commitment one way or the other. Later, when he was confronted with an adversary like Goldman who had arranged his "intellectual, emotional and ethical feelings . . . into some kind of coincidence," his equivocation looked foolish. Former friends, like Russo, watched his position be refuted by the opinion of Goldman. Former detractors, like Mrs. Hanna, were more firmly convinced that he lacked leadership.

Foley suffered a personal disaster, in terms of his reputation and personal affection, as a result of his equivocation. As a state education commissioner, he competed for the attention of teachers and citi-

[2] Cf., Richard Neustadt's prescription for presidential power; ". . . to induce as much uncertainty as possible about the consequences of ignoring what he wants." *Presidential Power,* p. 64. The immoderate litigant would seem to supply as much "uncertainty" as the political system can bear.

zens with local school boards, irate parents, educational critics, educators in the national and state governments, and private educational groups—even university presidents. In one evasive moment he lost whatever competitive advantage he possessed in Midland. Thereafter, his aspirations to accomplish important things would be far more likely to be frustrated until this disaster somehow could be redeemed. No school board was likely to defer to a man who was a "chicken," whose positions were "unspeakable," who "never says what [he] thinks," who talked "doubletalk," and who was unwilling to get embroiled in an unpopular issue. If he were to get the Board in a tough spot, he might leave it dangling and, as Woodford put it, "not help us out at all."

The law forces an official to be a leader or a fool. One does not equivocate in the immediate vicinity of a law suit.

Every school administrator in Midland, large or small, had at some time or another undergone an experience analogous to Foley's, and the memory of such a personal debacle was a spur to resolving long-standing inconsistencies. They knew that the protection of other goals depended upon their personal reputations for decisiveness.[3]

A Trustworthy Environment: Voluntarism

What determined the direction in which the equivocation was resolved? Of all the factors within the Midland educational organization, the most crucial was the informal group with which the individual official was affiliated.

The Midland school board was limited to seven persons, with solidarity and high morale.

The principals as a group were too many and too variegated to derive the same degree of mutual enjoyment as the school board. There were various friendship cliques, however, consisting of the Jews, of the spinsters, of the men, of the principals within a particular section of town, of the heads of the laboratory schools (where practice teachers from Teachers' College instructed). Miss Barrone had a long-standing Spanish study group with three of her colleagues. Several were members of the same honorary society. Service together on the standing committees of the Principals' Club turned acquaintances into friends. Some of the younger administrators first taught in schools led by veteran principals, and their friendships had endured.

[3] Cf., *Brehm and Cohen,* p. 228: "Cognitive dissonance is a general 'motivational state' that always occurs when there is some prior motive associated with the cognitions that are dissonant."

A few of the principals remained outside the system's informal organization, but the loners were surprisingly scarce. Only four[4] had no close friends within the school system itself. The fifteen remaining principals, in varying degrees, liked other educators well enough to want to be with them outside the daily routine. This social tendency to want to associate informally with trusted friends is called voluntarism. We call a group voluntarist when its members understand that every other member can freely withdraw at any time without excessive disadvantages.

In any small group of friends there is a commitment to stay together. Each member has a stake in maintaining pleasantry and in keeping the group going. The rewards of friendship justify compromises. With trustworthy comrades working in the same profession, a Midland official had a chance to relax and to talk shop indiscreetly, knowing his confidence would be kept. He took solace from people who saw his troubles as he did, and received praise from friends who shared his triumphs.

Within each of these voluntarist groups there were forces tending to disintegration: divisive issues unexpectedly intruded, and decisions over the allotment of group time to one subject or another produced friction. To protect the group from fragmentation, its members worked centripetally, agreeing on the need to get agreement, to have unity.

Each of the informal voluntarist groups within the system in its turn worked for, enjoyed, and lauded itself for its little unities. When a divisive issue intruded, every member pitched in to define a common meeting point on which all his friends could converge to form a practical unanimity.

Within the friendship group, however, each partner was also an adversary, wanting collective agreement which was as close to his own starting point as possible. In this mixed adversary-friend situation, a potential meeting place which was qualitatively unique had an irresistible attraction. It was not that a particular unique focal point was substantively the most attractive to the majority of the members; indeed, all members of the group might be unhappy with it. But the strongest argument for accepting a unique point of compromise was the rhetorical question[5] "If not here, then where?" The law in the *Schempp* case

[4] Cagney, Mareno, Miss O'Brien, and Woodford scored less than two on the four-point Social Activities Index.

[5] Thomas C. Schelling, *The Strategy of Conflict* (Cambridge, Mass.: Harvard University Press, 1960), p. 65.

was just such a focal point. No doubt it was satisfactory to very few members of the Midland school system, but members of the small groups could find no other single point of coordination. Some point of agreement had to be reached before the small group fragmented or the threatened law suit materialized, and the rule of *Schempp,* almost by default, won the day in one informal group after another. After all, if the agreement was not at the separatist point designated by the Supreme Court, where else could it be? Add to the pressing need for agreement the fact that some of these groups contained an educator whose original separatist convictions had been vindicated by the prayer case and whose determination to stand up for her rights was clear to her friends in the group, and it is not overly difficult to see the possibility of widespread agreement to comply, although initially the majority of persons in the organization opposed compliance.[6]

Barnard points out that small informal groups function within an organization to maintain a zone of indifference. In the Midland school system, such was the case. The member of the small informal group who modified his attitudes in accordance with *Schempp* was compensated by his fellows with both praise and gratitude redeemable in the future. Mrs. Hanna noted, for example, that Rizzuto "played the game, and he decided with us." Because the school board was an ongoing informal group, a compromising member like Rizzuto could count on his colleagues to reciprocate on some other issue in the future.

If an informal group had been together for a long time and had attained unity on a series of issues, the experience of solidarity increased the self-confidence of its members. Whenever one member persuaded an accommodating friend to accept his attitude, the persuading partner hardened his own convictions. Goldman, for example, suggested as a gimmick the formation of a committee to study and improve the teaching of moral values. When he convinced Rizzuto and Mrs. Hanna, however, Goldman began to think better of his own idea. The willingness of members in a productive small informal group to accommodate their fellows worked a kind of self-persuasion, eliminating doubts and reducing equivocation.

[6] This analysis draws heavily on Thomas C. Schelling, *The Strategy of Conflict* (Cambridge, Mass.: Harvard University Press, 1960), especially his third chapter, "Bargaining, Communications and Limited War," pp. 53-80. This brilliant book seems to have universal relevance to human affairs, big and small, from coping with atomic bombs or intractable children to negotiating the traffic or the con men in Times Square.

Within these groups of trustworthy persons, mutually desiring to find a point of agreement on any divisive issue, the Midland official aired his deepest convictions on the matter of schoolhouse religion. He unashamedly let his equivocations rise to the surface, where they were examined by his friends. In resolving his own inconsistencies, he listened to their "guidance" without feeling diminished by his dependence on their help.

Visualize, for example, the always vocal principal Miss Mercer listening to her troubled and apolitical friends Miss Battistella and Miss FitzGerald. Then, as the conversational initiative returned to her, she gently filled in for them the historical background of the Court's positions on separation of church and state; (not only could she draw on her own considerable knowledge, but she also took notes on Goldman's remarks and had memorized them). She began by admitting, woman to woman, her own misgivings about the *Schempp* case (for example, she agreed with Miss Battistella that the public school prayer ban might encourage Catholic parents to place their children into parochial institutions), but as she continued she introduced the bright side. After all, the new program of character education might be successful; the firm stand of the board prevented public upheaval; and news media were generally favorable to the prayer ban; the Midland school system, in other matters, was really going places; and so forth. In this trusting, unthreatening, and pleasant association, the overcoming of the resistance to change was begun.

The Tools

What happened to the participants in these intimate conversations? The principal contribution of these informal talks was to provide officials important intellectual tools. These tools permitted the individuals to accept the Supreme Court decision and at the same time to preserve undamaged the absolute maximum of their old attitude structures. Miss O'Hara remarked on the origins of the sharp verbal distinction which had enabled her to accept the fact that the Court's separatism and the teacher's obligation to her pupils were compatible.

> Being Catholic, I could not make a distinction between guidance and prayer. I did not see how I would still be free to function as I had as a guide after the board policy . . . Dr. Bartkowicz pointed out I could still. As a school person I gave a great deal of guidance to individuals, and it had a religious bent to it . . . But Dr. Bartkowicz saw no reason why I could not still function in a moral guidance position

to the individual student, because the rule was only that students as a group could not participate in a prayer ritual at the school.

This differentiation between guidance and prayer was of the utmost consequence to Miss O'Hara. Without it, she faced the dilemma of disobedience or demoralization, of being a bad citizen or a bad teacher. With the opportunity to talk matters out with her co-religionist Dr. Bartkowicz, the dilemma dissolved.

I have already spoken, in Chapter VI, of differentiation. By partly redefining familiar concepts, the individual distinguished between philosophy and religion, between individual prayers and collective prayers, between manners and meditation, and between guidance to individuals and ritual. Small groups provided the social areas in which there took place this process of breaking up previously unitary concepts into their good and bad components.

Differentiation was not the only intellectual tool developed in these intimate conversations among friends. Recall the discussion of the technique of sweet lemons, the drawing of new implications from old attitudes. The interviews provided at least one striking instance of a small group consensually arriving at a reinterpretation of a prior attitude. In the small group composed of the school board and superintendents, eight of the nine participants expressed a variation of Rizzuto's theme.

As I say, it's purely hypothesis now, but I have a feeling that the concern that has been occasioned by the necessity to fill the vacuum in character education will have a very good effect. I think this will be very salutary.

That is, the prayer ban, in the short run, did produce bad effects (old attitude), but concern about the bad effects, in the long run and in terms of the quality of family life and of school curriculum, has been very salutary (the sweet lemon twist). In small groups whose members wished to preserve their solidarity, such Candide-like techniques were well received.

A third intellectual device disseminated within friendship groups was remedial reanalysis. The official reexplained why his old beliefs were true. For example, the realist Miss Barrone re-searched the causal connection between schoolhouse prayers and the strengthening of underprivileged children. She came to the conclusion that the most important effect of prayer was that it tended to calm middle-class teachers, who consequently were more patient with their students.

With this analysis of the causalities involved, Miss Barrone had begun to look for other ways to bolster the teacher's strength. In small groups articulate researchers such as Miss Barrone tended to dominate conversation.[7]

Differentiation, sweet lemons, remedial research—in common these intellectual tools involved reanalysis of concepts, values, and relationships. In the decentralized privacy of friendship groups, the reanalysis was made; and when it was completed for each individual, the relief from the pressure of equivocation was very pleasant.

External Protection

A man's attitudes are not neutral, but affect others. His friends and neighbors come to rely on the stability of his inclinations.

Attitude change toward schoolhouse religion, imminent or completed, threatened the status quo, and invariably these reliant friends and neighbors took countervailing action: they retaliated, they blackmailed, they entreated, they tried to make the change so costly to the individual that he would return to the fold. Just as Goldman cajoled Mayor Fiorito back to his original position of support for the Court, so the Midland community external to the school system worked to reinstate the unionist and near-unionist orthodoxy the officials had previously shared.

Of course, in the medical analogy to which the educators tended to turn, there is nothing comparable to restoring a once-excised attitude. Nonetheless, the analogy serves to focus on the damage done by defensive overexertions too soon after a successful attitude change.

Chapter VI asserted that the nulists were never able to cope with the assaults within their social circles when they tentatively tried the new separatist attitudes. The challenge of this social denunciation was too severe for Dr. Clancy, Miss Barber, or Miss Battistella, and they retreated. Loss of comradeship and pleasantry, then, was one effective cost the external community could inflict.

Another cost was diminution of political status. The politician Farley and the seven other professionals (i.e., the liberateds and reverse liberateds), had a stake in the cooperative relationships they

[7] Some of the most illuminating inquiry into the persuasive effects of an individual within a small social group stems from the so-called 'jury studies.' See Fred L. Strodtbeck, Rita M. James, and Charles Hawkins, "Social Status in Jury Deliberations," *American Sociological Review,* 22 (1957), 713-19.

had established with their colleagues and their neighborhoods. These officials had to worry about jeopardizing this hard-won political goodwill. It was extremely vulnerable to attack.

Third, attitude change had economic implications. Irate parents and teachers had the option of removing their children to suburban public schools or to Midland parochial and private schools, thereby diminishing a sizeable part of the business of Midland's school system.

Fourth, there was physical jeopardy from the persons who took the law into their own hands. Rynne, the former athlete, told a story of one father who "came in waving his fist at me and said he was going to accompany his son to school and they would get down on their knees in the classroom and pray." While this unrestrained parent was not as dangerous as a bomb threat, a few disruptions in the classroom like this could well have wrecked the morale of Rynne's junior high school.

In sum, when an official changed his attitude on the issue of school house prayers, he incurred certain social, political, economic, and physical dangers which he could avoid if he recanted. If law was to be effective in inducing permanent psychological change, it had to provide a benign, post-operative environment where the individual needed only to flex his muscles, not depend on them for his very life.

In Midland, the legal system was at least in part successful in providing protection. Its first assistance was largely negative. The lawyers, at least the prominent ones, did not divide on the issue. The profession looked monolithic, despite the fact that an election campaign highlighted the legal issue. The newsworthy lawyers acted in concert behind Goldman. As a result, whenever irate citizens looked for legal and philosophical weapons to hurl at some vulnerable official, they found none, at least in the legal realm. Without a news maker sufficiently expert to define the portents of the prayer ban, social retaliation flagged.

The second device was that law had national application, and invited vindicated citizenry simultaneously and in every town to enforce it. Thus, while the prayer ban conceivably disadvantaged Midland, the school systems of Chicago and Cleveland suffered the same handicap concomitantly. The old saying about garlic eaters, "An odor common to both is offensive to none," applies as well to the law.[8]

[8] The doctrine of relative disadvantage has had more deft articulation. See particularly R. K. Merton and A. Kitt, "Contributions to the Theory of Reference Group Behavior," in R. K. Merton and P. F. Lazarsfeld (eds.),

As a matter of fact, however, the law was not invoked uniformly. Both Midland suburbs, Northland and Milltown, resisted the prayer cases without incurring the costs of a civil suit. It was a fortuity that Midland as a locality had sufficient unrelated advantages to compensate for this legal discrimination. In an evenly matched competition, however, the disparity might have invited backlash, for the effect was to give the lawbreaker a relative advantage over the compliant.

So, too, with the Midland private parochial and non-sectarian schools. If, in fact, the public and private schools had been in closer competition, the prayer ban, with its application limited to governmental schools, might have worked invidiously. The public and private schools were not competitive, however, because the government retained the significant advantage of providing education free of charge. It enjoyed a monopoly of gratuitous schooling. While even-handed enforcement of the law is essential, it need exist only for effective competitors.

Finally, the political elite, with control over the instruments of public order, were ready to punish lawbreakers within Midland itself. Criminal retaliation against the law-abiding never became a serious threat, because punishments by the guardians of the public order were so certain and so severe. It was not even thinkable, except in the single incident Rynne related.

Unanimity among legal spokesmen, even-handed enforcement of the law among competitors, certain punishment for the illegal posse—these factors ameliorated the Midland environment in which the school system was set. Without the law's protection, however, the compliant, gently nursing his new feelings, would have had to reverse his legal commitment. There was too much else at stake to be left dangling in the open.

Concluding Hypotheses

Two major propositions can be drawn from the facts of this study. The first pertains to the factors, both social and psychological, which tend to bring about legal compliance. The second generalization catalogues some of the results, social and psychological, of an individual's

---

Continuities in Social Research (Glencoe, Ill.: Free Press, 1950), pp. 40-105 —for example: "The degree to which a person is satisfied with a given state of affairs may be determined not necessarily by his absolute level of achievement or benefit, but instead by how much he achieves or benefits relative to those around him."

commitment to comply with law. Here in summary fashion is a statement of some of the causes and consequences of law-abidingness.

The likelihood of commitment to legal compliance is greater,

the more diverse the range of social groups with which one associates. This has been shown with regard to the professionals' (i.e., the liberateds and reverse liberateds) committing themselves to eventual compliance.

the higher proportion of vindicateds in one's social groups. This has been shown with regard to the school board and superintendents, who chose to comply more readily than the principals.

the greater the unanimity among newsworthy lawyers on the importance of compliance. This has been shown with regard to the principals' sensitivity to the reactions of prominent lawyers.

the more access one has to lawyers. This has been shown with regard to the school board and superintendents, who chose to comply more readily than the principals.

the more political leaders with status commit themselves to comply. This has been shown with regard to the professionals' (i.e., the liberateds and reverse liberateds) committing themselves to eventual compliance.

the graver the danger of legal action and more probable the invocation of judicial review in the event of non-compliance. This has been shown with regard to the professionals (i.e., the liberateds and reverse liberateds) and their concern about a disruptive law suit brought by a minority group.

the less grave and the less likely the danger of extralegal retaliation against thc compliant. This has been shown with regard to the permanence of the converts' commitment to comply relative to the instability of the nulists' commitment.

the deeper the identification with the social organization which commits itself to compliance. This has been shown with regard to the professionals' (i.e., the liberateds and the reverse liberateds) committing themselves to eventual compliance.

the greater the prestige of the lawmaker. This has been shown with regard to the compliance of those originally holding positive attitudes about the Supreme Court.

the more verbally sophisticated the individual. This has been shown with regard to the converts' successful adoption of the Supreme Court's concepts.

the greater the individual's willingness to learn. This has been shown with regard to Miss Barrone's acceptance of the lawmaker in contrast to Berman's and Miss FitzGerald's rejection.

the more heightened the individual's sense of volition. This has been shown with regard to the school board and superintendents, who chose to comply more readily than the principals.

the less the discrepancy between the original self-image and the legally prescribed self-image. This has been shown with regard to the patriots' greater frequency of compliance relative to the trustees and the unionists.

the less time available to the individual to resist the lawmaker. This has been shown with regard to the converts' committing themselves to comply.

The commitment to comply tends to be followed by

a search for informational support of compliance. This has been shown with regard to the converts, who read about the Court.

a search for social support of compliance. This has been shown with regard to the school board members, who increased the solidarity of their group.

individual effort to influence others in a compliant direction. This has been shown with regard to the liberateds' acting in small groups.

appreciation of former adversaries. This has been shown with regard to the liberateds' and the converts' understanding the original position of the vindicateds.

retaliation by former friends. This has been shown with regard to the treatment of the school board.

sub-conscious hostility to old loyalties. This has been shown inferentially with regard to the reverse liberateds', before *Schempp,* perceiving themselves as irreligious upon their commitment to separatism.

overreaction. This has been shown with regard to the extreme skepticism expressed by some converts for their original position.

an increased sense of freedom of action. This has been shown with regard to the converts' toleration of minor infractions of the letter of the law.

increasing commitment to comply. This has been shown with regard to the converts' increasing vigor in defending their compliance as they encountered more opposition.

an increased respect for the lawmaker. This has been shown with regard to the positive feelings for the Supreme Court which the liberateds, reverse liberateds, and converts developed.

The Significance

Judge Learned Hand, late of the federal Court of Appeals, once cautioned:

> I often wonder whether we do not rest our hopes too much upon constitutions, upon laws and upon courts. These are false hopes; believe me, these are false hopes. Liberty lies in the hearts of men and women; when it dies there, no constitution, no laws, no court can save it; no constitution, no law, no court can even do much to help it. While it lies there it needs no constitution, no law, no court to save it.[9]

Because Judge Hand is so highly regarded, because his premise of legal inefficacy runs through the controversy regarding judicial activism and restraint,[10] and because analysis of what he said brings out the importance of this study, it warrants examination.

"The spirit of liberty" Hand defines as "the spirit which is not too sure that it is right."[11] It is tolerance, empathy, compromise, compassion, humility—in short, a certain kind of deep-rooted attitude, to use the language of the present study.

According to Judge Hand, such profound attitudes can not be shaped by legal institutions. The family, education, friends and experience will create and preserve such attitudes, but not law. We need only to reflect on the experience of the backlashers and the nulists to recognize the wisdom contained in Hand's caution.

There are, however, two fallacies in Hand's argument. First, while it is true that law is unlikely to save any important attitudes if it is solidly opposed by all other social institutions, the same holds true of any institution which breeds moral attitudes—the churches and the schools, for example—which also would be unable to preserve a spirit of liberty if it were alone in a hostile world. Where there is no monolithic trend, however, where the population is ambivalent or indecisive or divided, where the life or death of a deep-rooted attitude is still uncertain, then legal institutions can and apparently do shore up the partisans (or detractors) of that attitude. For every situation where all institutions disintegrate at once (as Hand's remarks presuppose),

[9] Learned Hand, *The Spirit of Liberty* (New York: Vintage, 1959), p. 144.

[10] Including Judge Hand's *The Bill of Rights* (Cambridge, Mass.: Harvard University Press, 1958). See, among others, Charles L. Black, Jr., *The People and the Court* (New York: Macmillan, 1960) (judicial activism), and Herbert Wechsler, "Toward Neutral Principles of Constitutional Law," *Harvard Law Review,* 73 (1959), 1-34 (judicial restraint).

[11] Hand, *The Spirit of Liberty,* p. 144.

there are a dozen marginal situations where opposing factions are nearly equal and where a small but decisive factor (such as a legal decision) can make a difference.

Which leads to the second fallacy, the fallacy of ignoring contexts. Hand wrote, "While [the spirit of liberty] lies [in the hearts of men], it needs no constitution, no law, no court to save it." It depends.

If a tolerant man exists in circumstances where unless legal institutions can protect him he will suffer the loss of his dignity, friends, or customers if he behaves tolerantly, then Judge Hand is wrong when he observes that law is unnecessary to save the spirit of liberty. As a general proposition there are some circumstances (such as the tolerant man in the intolerant society) where law is both necessary and effective in shaping and preserving deep-rooted attitudes.

These two fallacies I call the Fallacies of Cataclysm and Overabstraction. The Fallacy of Cataclysm refers to ignoring the importance of small factors in a state of near equilibrium. The Fallacy of Overabstraction refers to ignoring the differences in social contexts in which persons live. Hand was too wise an observer of the human condition to have committed these fallacies unwittingly; he was urging a point by overstating it. Nonetheless, his cautionary words about placing too many hopes in the law have given some succor to those who have resisted recent legal changes begun by legislatures and, particularly, by the Supreme Court of the United States. To set things aright, I would restate Judge Hand's caution in light of some of the findings of this study.

Judge Hand might have said:

> I often wonder, what are the circumstances under which we may rest our hopes upon constitutions, law, and courts. This is a formidable social question which lawmakers have to understand. Liberty depends upon heartfelt attitudes of men and women; in circumstances where there are no institutions to mediate between law and those people who harbor doubts about democratic attitudes, the law is rendered ineffectual. We can and should take steps to assure that such circumstances never occur by promoting numerous voluntary associations, social pluralism, better education, the upgrading of lawyers, and the training of judges. If these latter conditions obtain, then constitutions, laws, and courts can do their part—their highly flexible part—to engraft and preserve the attitudes upon which liberty depends.

The importance of this point cannot be overstated: law can have widespread effect on deep-rooted attitudes.

At the same time, law is a sensitive social tool. Ineptly used, it produces backlash. Even properly used, law causes friction when it encounters a contrary community opinion, which wears away the reputation of lawmakers. This damage to the goodwill of legal institutions has to be calculated in counting the costs of employing the law to alter widely held social attitudes.

Awareness that law is a delicate tool does not, however, imply its need for overprotection. Factors exist in American society which strengthen the effectiveness of legal institutions. The first is the development of an organized law profession, with professional standards and national training, a body of lawyers which can and sometimes does act in concert to support lawmakers. Among the profession is a growing number of respected lawyers strongly identified with the lawmaking institutions. In the development of this identification a factor of importance is the experience young lawyers get as clerks to federal and state judges. If Goldman is typical, a youthful apprenticeship to the judiciary results in an enduring loyalty.

Second, there is the tradition of written judicial opinions and their dissemination. The judicial opinion, in conjunction with judicial review of legislation, contains a description and justification of the action of lawmakers and bureaucrats. Thus, in effect, judges are made the spokesmen for legal institutions in general, and publication of their opinions gives them as such spokesmen a communication initiative that is comparable to the advantage a president of the United States enjoys when he uses his press conferences effectively. The idiom of the judicial opinion shapes the idiom of political debate. Language, we have observed, facilitates attitude change, and in the molding of attitudes the written judicial word, widely published in a literate society, has a substantial influence.

The third advantage is that American legal institutions have been organized so that the concerned private citizen can invoke and indirectly enforce the law. The threat of law does not depend entirely, or even in large part, upon the whim of bureaucrats. Rather, as was the fact in *Schempp,* enforcement of law comes by way of a civil action, brought by persons and interest groups seeking civil, not criminal, remedies. The subtlety of the common law procedure may be that it puts the responsibility for calling the law into effect in the lap of the private citizen with a stake in the matter. To sharpen the point: perhaps one reason for the ineffectiveness of Prohibition was its dependence for enforcement upon criminal means exclusively. No private rights to invoke judicial power in its name were created.

The organization of the legal profession, the written judicial opinion, and the tradition of the civil remedy—these three distinctively legal factors, coupled with the social factors of pluralism, voluntarism, and literacy, account in large part for the potential power of the law in the United States.

We return to our initial question: Can law change deep-rooted attitudes? Of course it can. It has done so—in reshaping in less than a generation this nation's views about racism; in altering in even a shorter time police attitudes toward criminal behavior; in ennobling the city dweller as the backbone of Amercan democracy; in imparting an understanding of poverty; in recasting our ideas about leisure; in maintaining certain attitudes of good sportsmanship apparently essential to a competitive market economy; in stemming religious prejudice; in establishing heightened standards of honesty and public service. Indeed, it is hard to think of any widely held attitude upon which law has not had a significant influence: our attitudes about loyalty, sex, privacy, honesty, responsibility, innovation, democracy, freedom, tolerance, progress, patriotism, economics, and of course religion have all been affected by the legal context within which we live. Judiciously used, law can and does manipulate our deep-rooted attitudes, our personalities.

Is it good, this capacity for law to affect attitudes? Is it wise to show lawmakers how they may use law to effect widespread and calculated attitude change? Presumably by increasing the lawmaker's understanding of the process of legal change, we enlarge his effectiveness to manipulate the circumstances under which minds can be controlled. If such an implication sounds sinister, so much the better to be forewarned against the abuses of law.

It must also be remembered, however, as Herbert Kaufman reminds us, that "that which is called control of the mind is, when viewed from another standpoint, also termed morality."[12] If law can teach, can inculcate, can widen and deepen the citizen's humanity, then knowledge of how law works is an indispensable step in using legislation to produce better citizens. Moreover, making the knowledge of its effects available to all, instead of leaving insight into it the monopoly of a few, protects against the misuses of law. Thus, widespread knowledge of how our society works is both the accelerator of social change and at the same time its most effective brake. At least, such is the assumption of social science.

[12] Herbert Kaufman, *The Forest Ranger* (Baltimore: Johns Hopkins University Press, 1960), p. 233.

Methodological Postscript

This study is not the product of preconceived notions of how law changes attitudes. I had no assumptions of what the prayer ban would do to Midland teachers' views of schoolhouse religion, because I had no idea what their views were in the first place. The religious typology—unionist, trustee, patriot, and separatist—was not predefined when the interviewing began. As a consequence, there were no key questions to make the concepts operational, automatically sorting out each interviewee into his appropriate type. The typology created itself, so to speak, out of the data and after the development of the questionnaire—out of the "help" and "do not hurt" imagery the educators themselves employed and, further, out of the neutralist or belligerent posture of those aligned in the "do not hurt" camp.

The point made here is that conceptualization and operationalization of certain key concepts were made simultaneously and after the fact—had to have been so made, I would maintain, because of the dearth of earlier political theory in the area. The point applies to such crucial concepts as discrepancy and congruency between thought and action, the equivocalness of cognitions about the law, the kinds of leadership, the researcher and the uneducable personality, freedom, commitment, responsibility, and coercion. This combination of *post hoc* conceptualization and makeshift operationalization gives this study a degree of methodological looseness which should challenge the reader to question both the findings and the generalizations.

In the text and appendix I have tried to be as explicit as possible in describing the method of content analysis devised to operationalize the concepts employed, but no interjudge reliability tests were utilized. I would be the first to admit that I frequently created and employed a method because its results corroborated conclusions I had previously intuited.

If I were to pick out the methodologically weakest part of this study (but substantively the most crucial and, to me, the most convincing), it would be the process of congruency—the process by which an original equivocation resolves itself unequivocally after it has been put into issue. This process was traced both with respect to the equivocation between thought and action over schoolhouse religion and with respect to the original judgmental receptivity toward information about the Supreme Court. In neither case was the original discrepancy or the ultimate congruency satisfactorily proved. I asserted (but never proved) that a so-called stigma (or exposure or commonplace) policy preference corresponded with a unionist (or trustee or patriot) self-image. Likewise, in the case of attitudes toward legal institutions, an examination of my method of measuring equivocation (as described in the Appendix) will show the absence of a definitive logic in the counting process.

Such methodological makeshift, I would insist, is justifiable and appropriate in venturing into a field not previously studied. At the same time, however, I would be seriously disappointed if the conclusions of this study went unchallenged and unchanged, for they only hint at the full explanation of the formation and modification of important political attitudes.

In this confessional and hopeful frame of mind, let me identify those concepts which plead for more adequate operationalization than I have given them.

Degrees of educability, or willingness to research.[1]

Degrees of verbal skills, or casuistry potential.

Degrees of discrepancy between the thought and action elements of an attitude.

Degrees of equivocation of feeling (both the ambivalence of feeling and the depth of experience have to be gauged to get to the judgmental/dissonance distinction).

Obviously, development of almost all the concepts made explicit

[1] As distinguished from the open "judgmental processing" mind and the closed "dissonance processing" mind.

in the summary section of Chapter VIII should be undertaken. But scholars have been more aggressive in dealing with the importance of the social context in which one lives and the prestige of the communicator, to take two examples, than of the four factors mentioned above, which now deserve some compensating priority of effort.

Appendix A: Personnel

School Board

VINCE RIZZUTO. Chairman, educational aids specialist, former teacher; age in forties; Roman Catholic; liberal, registered Democrat; unionist, reverse liberated. Portrait, pp. 23–24.

TIMOTHY CLANCY. Pediatrician; age forty; Roman Catholic; conservative; unionist, nulist. Portrait, pp. 63–64.

BEN COLEMAN. Social worker; age thirty-nine; Protestant; conservative; unionist, convert. Portrait, pp. 40–41.

NATHAN DERZON. Retailer, former teacher; age forty-one; Jewish; liberal; separatist, vindicated.

FRANK GOLDMAN. Lawyer; age forty-four; Jewish; liberal, registered Democrat; separatist, vindicated. Portrait, pp. 113–20.

MRS. KATHERINE HANNA. University professor; age fifty-one; Protestant; liberal; separatist, vindicated.

CALVIN LEONARD. Manufacturer; former teacher; age forty-seven; Congregationalist; liberal; separatist, vindicated. Portrait, pp. 24–25.

Superintendents

JOHN BARTKOWICZ. Superintendent; age in early fifties; Roman Catholic; liberal; patriot, convert. Portrait, pp. 26–28.

MISS MARY O'HARA. Associate superintendent; age in late sixties; Roman Catholic; liberal, registered Republican; patriot, reserve liberated. Portrait, pp. 28–30.

Principals

Senior High Schools

PETER MARENO. Age fifty-seven; Roman Catholic; conservative; unionist, backlasher.

TOM MURPHY. Previous president of Teachers' Association; age fifty-nine; Roman Catholic; middle of the road; patriot, liberated. Portrait, p. 104.

Junior High Schools

HAROLD BERMAN. Age fifty-seven; Jewish; conservative; unionist, backlasher. Portrait, pp. 35, 43.

JAMES RYNNE. President of Teachers' Association; age forty-five; Roman Catholic; middle of the road; trustee, liberated. Portrait, pp. 38–39.

Elementary Schools

MISS ANN BARBER. Age sixty; Roman Catholic; middle of the road; unionist, nulist. Portrait, pp. 90–91.

MISS MARIE BARRONE. Age sixty-three; Roman Catholic; conservative; patriot, liberated. Portrait, pp. 31–33.

MISS LOUISE BATTISTELLA. Age fifty; Roman Catholic; conservative; unionist, nulist. Portrait, p. 49.

JOE CAGNEY. Age forty-eight; Roman Catholic; middle of the road; registered Republican; trustee, backlasher. Portrait, pp. 2–3.

MISS SARA COHEN. Age fifty-nine; Jewish; middle of the road; separatist, vindicated.

PAUL FARLEY. Age fifty-five; Roman Catholic; conservative; trustee; liberated. Portrait, pp. 44–45.

MISS BRENDA FITZGERALD. Age fifty-three; Roman Catholic; middle of the road; unionist, backlasher. Portrait, pp. 33–35.

MRS. MYRA GOLDBERG. Age sixty-one; Jewish; middle of the road; patriot, convert.

ISAIAH KAPLAN. Age fifty-eight; Jewish; liberal; separatist, vindicated. Portrait, pp. 43–44.

MISS JEAN KENNEDY. Age sixty-four; Roman Catholic; liberal; separatist, reverse liberated. Portrait, pp. 57–58.

MISS MARY MERCER. Age sixty-one; Roman Catholic; liberal; patriot, liberated. Portrait, p. 128.

MISS MOLLY O'BRIEN. Age sixty-six; Roman Catholic; middle of the road; unionist, nulist. Portrait, pp. 56–57, 91–93.

FRANK RUSSO. Successor president of the Teacher's Association; age thirty-five; Roman Catholic; middle of the road; unionist, convert. Portrait, pp. 39–40, 67–68.

MRS. CELESTE TORENO. Age forty-six; Roman Catholic; liberal, registered Democrat; patriot, convert.

CHARLES WOODFORD. Age thirty-seven; Episcopalian; liberal, registered Democrat; separatist, vindicated. Portrait, pp. 65–66.

Appendix B: Questionnaires

First Questionnaire, January-May, 1963

*1. How long have you lived in Midland?

*2. How long have you taught in Midland?

*3. How long have you been in school administration in Midland?

4. Do you like it? How do you like school administration?

5. I'm going to ask you now about your personal acquaintance with the Supreme Court of the United States. Do you remember learning about the Court and what it is supposed to do in our system of government, or not?

6. Some people tell me that they knew about the Court because someone in their family was a lawyer or a judge or a policeman. Was your grandfather or father or some close relative a lawyer or judge or policeman? Did he talk about the law? Favorably or unfavorably?

7. Is there anything in your lifetime that has happened which has made you more interested in the Supreme Court than usual, or not?

8. Some tell me that an experience in court—any court—has interested them in the law in general and the Supreme Court in particular. Were you ever at a trial—as a plaintiff, defendant, or witness, or in some other capacity such as spectator? Have you ever served on a jury?

9. In general, what do you think of the Supreme Court at present—as an institution or of the present personnel in particular?

10. Are there any Supreme Court decisions which stand out in your mind as being particularly notable, or not?

11. Now I want to ask you a couple of questions about what you think the Supreme Court ought to be and, then, what the President of the United States ought to be. Here is a card with twenty adjectives

* Asterisked questions were asked of the private school headmasters.

and phrases on it. First, which of these words come closest to describing your idea of what the Supreme Court ought to be?

1. courageous
2. conservative
3. partisan
4. liberal
5. cautious
6. widely popular
7. a moral example
8. busy
9. severe
10. tolerant
11. very influential
12. just
13. conscientious
14. sensitive to public opinion
15. idealistic
16. realistic
17. intellectual
18. wise
19. widely respected
20. aggressive

12. Now, using these same adjectives and phrases, can you select those words which come closest to describing your idea of what the President of the United States ought to be?

13. Which of these two statements comes closer to your own feelings:

a. If the Supreme Court makes a bad decision, it is its duty to admit its error and overrule itself as soon as possible.

b. If the Court makes an unpopular decision, it is up to the people to amend the Constitution if they do not agree with the decision, since the Court can only decide whether the Constitution forbids particular acts of government.

*14. Now, I am interested in the Supreme Court as it affects your work activities. And so I have selected a recent decision of the Court which in fact did affect people like yourself, but in another state. As you well know, last year parents of a few New York public schoolchildren objected to a short prayer which teachers had the children recite aloud at the start of each school day. The prayer was known as the Regents' Prayer, because it was composed by the New York State Board of Regents and was as follows: "Almighty God, we acknowledge our dependence upon Thee, and beg Thy blessings upon us, our parents, our teachers and our country." The Supreme Court of the United States ruled that New York public schoolteachers could not constitutionally have their students recite this Regents' Prayer in a public school classroom. That case was called *Engel v. Vitale.* It caused a furor then, and since that time there has been a lot of disagreement among interested people as to whether other forms of religious observance, such as the Lord's Prayer, are proper in the public schools, or not.

*15. In your own mind, do you think the Court prohibited other forms of religious observance in the public schools? What do you think the Court decided?

*16. Why do you think the Supreme Court decided the way it did?

*17. There seems to be a difference of opinion about the propriety of religious observances in public schools. As you see it, the difference of opinions is between whom—what kind of people would be against religious observances in public schools, and what kind would be for them?

*18. Do you see any obvious solution to reconciling this difference of opinion over religious observances in the public schools?

*19. Here are a few things that one might expect to happen if students were to have the opportunity to say prayers in school. Which of these do you think rather likely to happen because the opportunity is given to student to say prayers in school? (*Hand respondent card.*)

1. Some students might become better citizens.
2. Some students might become cynical about morals.
3. Some students might be more likely to become church members.
4. Some students might leave school with an inadequate idea of religion.
5. Some students might find it difficult to adjust to the religious practices of their parents.
6. Some teachers might have discipline problems in the classroom.
7. School spirit might increase.
8. Others.

*20. Now keep the card and, in your best guess, what do you think might be rather likely to happen if students were no longer given the opportunity to say prayers in school?

*21. As for giving an opportunity to students to say prayers in public schools, do you now think such a practice is right?

22. Here is a list of things or people from which we get considerable information about the world we live in. Did any of these help you to make up your mind as to how you felt about giving students the opportunity to say prayers in the public schools? (*Hand respondent card.*)

1. TV-radio news or commentary
2. Newspaper article or editorial
3. Magazine article
4. Book
5. President Kennedy
6. Somebody I talked with
7. Somebody I heard in person
8. Minister, priest, or rabbi
9. Newsreel
10. Professional association
11. Lawyer
12. Other

*23. In your own family, do you now say a prayer before meals daily or on special occasions?

*24. Were you given an opportunity to say prayers in your pre-college schools?

*25. Did you like or dislike saying prayers in school, or did it make no difference to you?

26. All things considered, in the decision that has to be made whether a public school student ought to be given an opportunity to pray together with his fellow students, who do you think would make the most-informed decision? Here is a card with five possible people or groups who could make that decision. Who is most likely to be best informed? Who is likely to be the next most informed? Who is least likely? Next least likely?

1. The individual homeroom teacher
2. Principal of the school
3. School board of the city
4. United States Supreme Court
5. Congress and the president.

*27. Now I should like to ask you a series of questions, all pertaining to particular forms of religious observances in your school. Would you like to have in your school any of these kinds of religious observance or not? You may answer that you would like to have it, dislike it, or that it would make no difference to you. Suppose a teacher required his class to recite aloud in the classroom a prayer, all students being required to say it. Would you like or dislike such a practice in your school?

*28. Now suppose that a teacher gives the class the opportunity to say prayers together in the classroom, any student who wishes being permitted to leave the room.

*29. How would you feel if the principal recited a prayer at morning assembly, any student remaining silent who wished to do so?

*30. How would you feel about the principal reading the Bible in morning assembly at Christmastime?

*31. What about a classroom teacher reading the Bible in his classroom at the beginning of each day, all students attending?

*32. Suppose the principal reads from the Bible daily in morning assembly, all students attending?

*33. Would you like or dislike the singing of hymns at Christmastime in morning assembly, all students being in attendance?

*34. How do you feel about the student body singing hymns daily in morning assembly, all students attending?

*35. What about a Bible-study course? Suppose one were required by the school board to be taught by the classroom teachers; would you like or dislike that requirement?

*36. If a Bible-study course were given as an option to a literature course and taught by a classroom teacher, how would you feel?

*37. And last, would you like an optional Bible-study course which was taught by a minister, priest, or rabbi, depending on the individual student's choice?

38. Let me ask you another hard question. In your best guess, what do you think the Supreme Court of the United States would think about these religious observances (qq. 27-37)? Would the Supreme Court find them constitutional or not? Let's start with the teacher who requires his class to recite aloud a prayer in the classroom, all students being required to say it . . .

39. Here is a card. *A*, *B*, and *C* are three attitudes which various groups and individuals in Midland take:

A. Expect me to *eliminate* daily prayers from my school/system.

B. Expect me to *give an opportunity* to students to pray in school.

C. Have *no expectations* regarding what I should do about prayers.

For each group or individual listed on this card, check that box or boxes which most nearly represents what they think about school prayers. (*Hand respondent card.*)

1. Politicians
2. Protestant groups
3. Catholic groups
4. Jewish groups
5. Business or commercial organizations
6. Labor unions
7. Parents (P.T.A.)
8. Teachers
9. Personal Friends
10. Police force
11. Individuals influential for economic reasons
12. Student opinion
13. Professional education associations
14. Service clubs
15. Fraternal organizations
16. Veterans organizations
17. Individual school board members
18. My family
19. The press
20. Bar associations
21. American Civil Liberties Union
22. Other

*40. In conversation with persons in education, certain subjects occur frequently. How do you personally feel about these opinions on these subjects? Do you agree or disagree? (*Hand respondent card.*)

a. Negroes should be integrated in every American public school, even if whites object intensely, even violently.

b. A man who serves in public office should have to declare a belief in God.

c. Dope addicts should be put in jail.

d. No school child should be required to recite the Pledge of Allegiance if he does not want to do so.

e. If an arrested man cannot afford a lawyer, the state should provide him one at the state's expense.

f. If a man deserts from the army in wartime, a suitable penalty would be to take away his American citizenship.

g. It seems only fair that parochial schools should get some form of governmental aid.

h. A community such as Midland should not be allowed to censor sacrilegious movies.

i. It seems hardly fair to bring children into the world with the way things look for the future.

*41. There is considerable disagreement about labor unions. With which of these four statements do you come closest to agreeing?

1. Labor unions in this country are dong a fine job.

2. While they do make some mistakes, on the whole labor unions are doing more good than harm.

3. Although we need labor unions in this country, they do more harm than good the way they are run now.

4. This country would be better off without any labor unions at all.

*42. Do you favor or oppose increasing expenditures to provide subsidized low-rent housing to those who cannot afford adequate housing of their own?

*43. People have told me that business enterprise can continue to give us our high standard of living only if it remains free from government regulation. In general how do you personally feel about this? (Agree? Disagree? Don't know?)

*44. Do you think you have more, the same, or less freedom to say and to believe things than was possible ten years ago? (People in general? Yourself personally?) (Why?)

*45. Have you ever been elected to office in a political party or in a political election for some governmental office?

*46. Are you a registered member of either political party at present?

*47. Religious preference?

*48. Last grade of education?

*49. Sex?

*50. Race?

*51. Occupation?

*52. In your school, do all teachers say prayers in the classroom?

Second Questionnaire, February-August, 1964

Last year, as you remember, I asked you about your feeling toward the American Supreme Court. I have had to come back to see you because after I finished my interviews the Court made a further decision in the area of public school prayers. As you know, in a case called *Abington Township v. Schempp,* the Supreme Court declared unconstitutional a Pennsylvania statute which required that public schools open each school day with a religious observance (e.g., the Lord's Prayer). Since the last part of my first interview with you dealt with the place of religion in the public schools, the *Schempp* case has obliged me to bring my study up to date. That is why I am here today, to catch up with events.

*1. Tell me, has your interest in the Supreme Court increased in the last year, or has it decreased? Have you read any books about it? Or any articles? Or have you found anything of interest elsewhere, say, on TV or in conversations?

*2. What about the *Schempp* opinion: did you ever read excerpts from it? Or the whole opinion? Where?

*3. In your own mind, what did the Court decide in *Schempp?*

*4. Why do you think the Court decided the way it did?

*5. Were you surprised by the decision or not?

*6. From what you know, is it likely that the Court will change its decision on the constitutionality of prayers in public school classrooms, or not?

7. What is the school board's present position on the matter of prayers in the classroom?

8. Why do you think it took the position it did?

9. Were you surprised that it took this position, or not?

10. Was it difficult for the school board to agree on this position, or do you think there was widespread agreement among board members beforehand, or not?

11. What do you think would have happened in the school system and in the community if the board had not taken the position it did after the Supreme Court rendered the *Schempp* decision?

12. How would you describe the reaction of the principals and the classroom staff to the school board's position? (For it? Against it? Divided?)

13. Were you surprised by any of their reactions?

*14. Here are a few things which one might expect to happen because of the new school board policy on prayers. Which of these is likely to happen because students no longer have the opportunity to say prayers in school? (*Hand respondent card*)

1. Some students are more likely to be better citizens under the new policy than under the old policy.

2. Some students are more likely to be cynical about morals under the new policy.

3. Some students are more likely to become church members under the new policy.

4. Some students will leave school with a less adequate idea of religion under the new policy.

5. Some students will find it more difficult to adjust to the religious practices of their parents under the new policy.

6. Some teachers will have more discipline problems in the classroom under the new policy.

7. School spirit is more likely to increase under the new policy.

8. Other.

15. As you see it, what are the probable effects in the school system of the ethics program which Dr. Bartkowicz's committee is formulating (the committee on moral values in the curriculum)?

16. What kind of public reaction was there to the school board decision? Why so?

17. (Question omitted after a few trials.)

18. What did you think of the position Mayor Fiorito took on the matter of religious observances? ("a moment of silent meditation at the beginning of the school day [as a way of giving] children an opportunity to develop moral and spiritual values").

19. What did you think of Commissioner Foley's position? (it should be in the "discretion" of the teacher whether there are prayers in the classroom).

20. Was the reaction of any other public person on this matter of interest to you? Who? What was his reaction? Anybody else?

21. Do you know any lawyers personally, or not? Well?

22. Did they express any opinions to you on public school prayers, or not? What were they?

23. Were you surprised by any of their reactions, or not?

Now I should like to ask you a series of questions, all pertaining to particular forms of religious observance that are possible in your school (system). Would you like to have in your school (system) any of these kinds of religious observance, or not? You may answer that you would like to have it, dislike it, or that it would make no difference to you.

*24. Suppose a teacher required his class to recite aloud in the classroom a prayer, all students being required to say it. Would you like or dislike such a practice in your school?

*25. Now suppose that a teacher gives the class the opportunity to say prayers together in the classroom, any student who wishes being permitted to leave the room.

*26. How would you feel if the principal recited a prayer at morning assembly, any student remaining silent who wished to do so?

*27. How would you feel about the principal reading the Bible in morning assembly at Christmastime? Would you like that or dislike it?

*28. What about a classroom teacher reading the Bible in his classroom at the beginning of each day, all students attending?

*29. Suppose the principal reads from the Bible daily in morning assembly, all students attending?

*30. Would you like or dislike the singing of hymns at Christmastime in morning assembly, all students attending?

*31. How do you feel about the students singing hymns daily in morning assembly, all students attending?

*32. If a Bible-study course were given as an elective in place of a literature course and taught by classroom teachers, how would you feel? Would you like it or dislike it?

*33. And last, would you like an elective Bible-study course which was taught by a minister, priest, or rabbi, depending on the individual student's choice?

*34. Now, as for giving an opportunity to students to say prayers in public schools, do you now think such a practice is right?

*35. Has any event—for example, the death of Pope John, or the civil rights demonstrations, or the assassination of President Kennedy—or some more private event, affected your thoughts on this matter in the last year?

36. As to the school board's decision on prayers, will there be any adverse effects to the public school system as a result of it? Beneficial effects?

37. I understand that in Northland the public school system is still giving children the opportunity to say prayers in school. Did you know that or not? What do you think of that? Any consequences for the Midland system?

38. Now, let me ask you something about your life away from school affairs. If you were to think of all the places outside the regular school routine where you are likely to see other public school colleagues—principals, teachers, superintendents (school board members) how often would you say that you see them in connection with matters other than school affairs? (Never? Less than once a month? Once or twice a month? Once or twice a week? Nearly every day?)

39. Do you ever visit any public school colleagues in their homes, or do any of them come to your home? If yes, would you say these visits occurred often, occasionally, or rarely?

40. With whom do you actually spend more of your free time—with public school colleagues or with friends who are not connected with the public school system?

41. In connection with the public school system, do you participate in any of these associations? To what degree?

a. Principals' Club
b. Teachers' Association
c. NEA
d. VFW Educators Post
e. Any other educational associations

42. As a final summary question, in regards to the Midland public school system, are you very satisfied with the progress the system is making, or very dissatisfied, or somewhere in between?

*43. I have asked you a lot of questions. Is there anything in connection with what we have been talking about about which I asked no questions but which you think important?

Appendix C: Indexes

The following indexes used in the text were constructed from the interview questions.

1. *Liberal-Conservative Index*

Q. 1-41 There is considerable disagreement about labor unions. With which of these four statements do you come closest to agreeing?

(1) Labor unions in this country are doing a fine job.
(2) While they do make some mistakes, on the whole they are doing more good than harm.
(3) Although we need labor unions in this country, they do more harm than good the way they are run now.
(4) This country would be better off without any labor unions at all.

(Dichotomized: (3), (4) or "Don't know" coded 0; (1) or (2) coded +1.)

Q. 1-42 Do you favor or oppose increasing expenditures to provide subsidized low-rent housing to those who cannot afford adequate housing of their own? (Dichotomized: "Oppose" or "Don't know" coded 0; "Favor" coded +1.)

Q. 1-43 People have told me that business enterprise can continue to give us our high standard of living only if it remains free from government regulation. In general how do you personally feel about this? (Dichotomized: "Agree" coded 0; "Disagree" or "Don't know" coded +1.)

The index was trichotomized between "liberal" (1), "middle of the road" (2), and "conservative" (3, 4). This three-item index is a modified version of a measure developed by Richard Centers in

The Psychology of Social Classes (Princeton: Princeton University Press, 1949).

	Distribution
CODE: 1. All those with score of +3	12
2. All those with score of +2	9
3. All those with score of +1	4
4. All those with score of 0	3
Total	28

2. *Social Activities Index*

Q. 2-38 If you were to think of all the places outside the regular school routine where you are likely to see other public school colleagues—principals, teachers, superintendents, school board members—how often would you say that you see them in connection with matters other than school affairs?

(1) Never?
(2) Less than once a month?
(3) Once or twice a month?
(4) Once or twice a week?
(5) Nearly every day?
(Dichotomized between "Once or twice a week," coded +1, and "Once or twice a month," coded 0.)

Q. 2-39 Do you ever visit any public school colleagues in their homes, or do any of them come to your home? If answer is yes, very often, occasionally, or rarely? (Dichotomized between "Very often," coded +1, and "Occasionally," coded 0.)

Q. 2-40 With whom do you actually spend more of your free time —with public school colleagues or with friends who are not connected with the public school system? (Dichotomized between "half and half," coded +1, and "not connected with," coded 0.)

Q. 2-41 In connection with the public school system, do you participate in any of these associations? If yes, to what degree?

(1) Principals' Club?
(2) Teachers' Association?
(Dichotomized between participation in both (1) and (2) and heavy participation in at least one, coded +1, and participation in only one or light participation in both (1) and (2), coded 0.)

This four-item index is a modified version of a measure developed by Seymour M. Lipset, Martin A. Trow and James S. Coleman in *Union Democracy* (Glencoe, Illinois: Free Press, 1956).

		Distribution
CODE:	1. All those with score of +4	8
	2. All those with score of +3	1
	3. All those with score of +2	8
	4. All those with score of +1	3
	5. All those with score of 0	8
	Total	28

3. *Religious Self-Image*

This measure was developed through content analysis of the interview material, but the following questions were central in characterizing the official as "Separatist," "Patriot," "Trustee" or "Unionist."

Q. 1-17 There seems to be a difference of opinion about the propriety of religious observances in public schools. As you see it, the difference of opinion is between whom—what kind of people would be against religious observances in public schools, and what kind would be for them?

Q. 1-19 Here are a few things that one might expect to happen if students were to have the opportunity to say prayers in school. Which of these do you think rather likely to happen because the opportunity is given to students to say prayers in school?

(1) Some students might become better citizens.

(2) Some students might become cynical about morals.

(3) Some students might be more likely to become church members.

(4) Some students might leave school with an inadequate idea of religion.

(5) Some students might find it difficult to adjust to the religious practices of their parents.

(6) Some teachers might have discipline problems in the classroom.

(7) School spirit might increase.

(8) Other.

Q. 1-20 In your best guess, what do you think might be rather likely to happen if students were no longer given the opportunity to say prayers in school? Alternatives (1) through (8), as in Q. 1-19.

Q. 2-14 Here are a few things which one might expect to happen because of the new school board policy on prayers. Which of these is likely to happen because students no longer have the opportunity to say prayers in school? Alternatives (1) through (8), as in Q. 1-19.

Q. 1-21)
2-34) As for giving an opportunity to students to say prayers in public schools, do you now think such a practice is right?

4. *Religious Policy Preference*

The following questions were asked with this preface: "Now, I should like to ask you a series of questions, all pertaining to particular forms of religious observances that are possible in your school (system). Would you like to have in your school (system) any of these kinds of religious observance, or not? You may answer that you would like to have it, dislike it, or that it would make no difference to you."

Q. 1-28)

2-25) Now suppose that a teacher gives his class the opportunity to say prayers together in the classroom, any student who wished being permitted to leave the room?

Q. 1-36)

2-32) If a Bible-study course were given as an option to a literature course and taught by a classroom teacher, how would you feel?

Q. 1-37)

2-33) Would you like an optional Bible-study course which was taught by a minister, priest, or rabbi, depending on the individual student's choice?

Q. 1-30)

2-27) How would you feel about the principal reading the Bible in morning assembly at Christmastime?

Q. 1-31/32)

2-28/29) How would you feel about a classroom teacher and/or the principal reading the Bible in the classroom and/or in morning assembly, all students attending?

Q. 1-34)

2-31) How do you feel about the student body singing hymns daily in morning assembly, all students attending?

Q. 1-27)

2-24) Suppose a teacher required his class to recite aloud in the classroom a prayer, all students being required to say it?

Q. 1-29)

2-26) How would you feel if the principal recited a prayer at morning assembly, any student remaining silent who wished to do so?

Q. 1-33)

2-30) Would you like or dislike the singing of hymns at Christmastime in morning assembly, all students being in attendance? (Each "Like" coded +1; each "Dislike" coded 0; each "Indifferent," coded 0 in the first interview and +1 in the second interview.)

This nine-item index, collapsed into three "sets," produced a Guttman cumulative-type scale, in which instead of using only one item to

		Distribution 1963	1964
CODE:	Q. 1-28) All those with +1	5	
	2-25)		7
	Q. 1-36) All those with +1	6	
	2-32)		13
	Q. 1-37) All those with +1	6	
	2-33)		5
	Q. 1-30) All those with +1	11	
	2-27)		7
	Q. 1-31/32) All those with +1	12	
	2-28/29)		6
	Q. 1-34) All those with +1	9	
	2-31)		6
	Q. 1-27) All those with +1	9	
	2-24)		7
	Q. 1-29) All those with +1	20	
	2-26)		16
	Q. 1-33) All those with +1	18	
	2-30)	—	21
	Total 1963 Interviews	96	—
	1964 Interviews		88

determine a given cutting point on the scale, as in the conventional procedure, three items were used. A score of +2 or more on any set of three items constituted a + for that set; otherwise a –. For a discussion of this modification of the conventional Guttman scale, see Samuel A. Stouffer, *Social Research to Test Ideas* (New York: Free Press of Glencoe, 1962), pp. 274-289, reprinted from Samuel A. Stouffer, Edgar F. Borgatta, David G. Hays, and Andrew F. Henry, "A Technique for Improving Cumulative Scales," *Public Opinion Quarterly,* 16 (1952), 273-291 (1952).

One might wonder why a preference for daily hymn singing (Q. 1-34/2-31 is more unionist than one for daily prayers (Q. 1-27/2-24). The answer rests in the largely Catholic composition of the interviewed population. To the Catholic respondents, hymns appeared to be prayers sung, hence were more sacredly charged than prayers said. To the Protestants, and perhaps to the Jews, hymns may well have been more secular. By and large, however, and given the preponderant Catholic character of the sample, I was convinced that most of the teachers saw daily hymn singing (as distinguished from carols) as having a more intrusive impact on the child than daily praying. The point to notice is that the same policy preference had widely differing significance, depending on the teacher's background, and shows the wisdom of the cumulative modification of the Guttman scale to offset the one-shot idiosyncrasy which frequently imperils the conventional one-item Guttman technique.

5. *Attitudes toward the Supreme Court, Courts, and Lawyers*

This measure of the character and intensity of feeling toward law-related persons was developed through content analysis of the interview material, but the following questions were central to the topic.

Q. 1-5 Do you remember learning about the Supreme Court and what it is supposed to do in our system of government?

Q. 1-6 Was your grandfather or father or some close relative a lawyer or judge or policeman?

Q. 1-7 Is there anything in your lifetime that has happened which has made you more interested in the Supreme Court than usual?

Q. 1-8 Were you ever at a trial, as a plaintiff, defendant, or witness or in some other capacity such as spectator? Have you ever served on a jury?

Q. 1-9 In general, what do you think of the Supreme Court at present?

Q. 1-10 Are there any Supreme Court decisions which stand out in your mind as being particularly notable?

Q. 2-1 Has your interest in the Supreme Court increased in the last year, or has it decreased?

Q. 2-4 Why do you think the Court decided the way it did (in *Schempp*)?

In both interviews, every sentence in which there was a reference to the Supreme Court, courts, or lawyers was valued as "favorable" or "unfavorable." In the first interview, the character of the feeling of the individual was determined by the character of the earliest memory of law-related events. The intensity of the feeling was determined as unequivocal if the number of favorable (or unfavorable, as the case might be) references exceeded the unfavorable (or favorable) references by at least five. In the second interview, the character was determined by the quantitatively predominant sentiment expressed in that interview, favorable or unfavorable. The intensity of the sentiment was determined as unequivocal if the aggregate number of favorable (or unfavorable) references in both the before and after interviews exceeded the unfavorable (or favorable) references by at least five.

Bibliographical Essay

Attitudes. The clearest, most useful conception of an attitude is found in M. J. Rosenberg, C. I. Hovland, *et al., Attitude Organization and Change* (New Haven: Yale University Press, 1960), especially in chapters 2 and 4. J. W. Brehm and A. R. Cohen provide in *Explorations in Cognitive Dissonance* (New York: John Wiley & Sons, 1962) a lucid summary of current research in cognitive dissonance, and their book contains a useful bibliography. In conjunction with the Brehm and Cohen book, one should read L. Festinger, *A Theory of Cognitive Dissonance* (Stanford: Stanford University Press, 1957), the stimulating first statement of the theory. One would do well also to read some of the alternative formulations, for example, F. Heider, *The Psychology of Interpersonal Relations* (New York: John Wiley & Sons, 1958), briefly summarized in F. Heider, "Attitudes and Cognitive Organization," *Journal of Psychology,* 21, (1946), 107-12. A special issue of the *Public Opinion Quarterly,* edited by D. Katz, "Attitude Change," 24 (1960), 163-365, is an immensely helpful summary and analysis of some of the various ways of looking at attitudes and attitude change.

American political attitudes were first systematically studied by Harold Lasswell in *Psychopathology and Politics* (Chicago: University of Chicago Press, 1930). The psychoanalytic explanation of political attitudes predominates in John Dollard *et al., Frustration and Aggression* (New Haven: Yale University Press, 1939), and T. W. Adorno *et al., The Authoritarian Personality* (New York: Harper & Bros., 1950). M. B. Smith, J. S. Bruner, and R. W. White in their *Opinions and Personality* (New York: John Wiley & Sons, 1956), by comparison, deemphasized the externalization aspect of political attitudes, and R. E. Lane's brilliant inquiry into the political beliefs of fifteen working-class men, *Political Ideology* (New York: Free Press of Glencoe, 1962), mentions social, economic, and intellectual explanations of their attitudes, almost exclusively of psychoanalytic explanations.

Attitude change induced by mass communications has been systematically studied and reported in a series of monographs edited by C. I. Hovland and published by the Yale University Press, among which is M. J. Rosenberg, C. I. Hovland, *et al., Attitude Organization and Change,* mentioned earlier. The study of innovation has produced useful generalizations with respect to attitude change, summed up in E. Katz, M. L. Levin, and H. Hamilton, "Traditions of Research on the Diffusion of Innovation," *American Sociology Review,* 28 (1963), 237 ff.; much of the basic research in diffusion stems from the rural sociologists, a useful summary of which is Herbert F. Lionberger, *Adoption of New Ideas and Practices* (Ames, Iowa: Iowa State University Press, 1960). Finally, one must mention Alexander H. Leighton, *The Governing of Men* (Princeton: Princeton University Press, 1946), for his study of the impact of American wartime regulation upon the belief systems of Japanese-American evacuees from the West Coast.

Men work in social groups, and the effect of such groups on men's attitudes is discussed in G. C. Homans, *The Human Group* (New York: Harcourt, Brace, 1950), and in the works of K. Lewin, for example, K. Lewin and P. Grabbe, "Conduct, Knowledge and the Acceptance of New Values," *Journal of Social Issues* (1945), 53-64. A useful concept which students of social groups have employed is role, or self-image, as I have called it in the present book. Two essays by Samuel A. Stouffer, "An Analysis of Conflicting Social Norms," *American Sociological Review,* 14 (1949), 707-17, and (with J. Toby), "Role Conflict and Personality," *American Journal of Sociology,* 56 (1951), 395-406, and a full-length book by N. Gross, W. S. Mason, and A. W. McEachern, *Explorations in Role Analysis* (New York: John Wiley & Sons, 1958), make some fruitful applications of the concept of role conflict; but in political science the concept of role seems to have had less successful application in J. C. Wahlke, H. Eulau, *et al., The Legislative System* (New York: John Wiley & Sons, 1962).

Social Organizations. My book owes much to two books. One is C. I. Barnard, *The Functions of the Executive* (Cambridge, Mass.: Harvard University Press, 1938), now more than a quarter of a century old and yet an indispensable book for the understanding of organization administration. The persons who have been influenced by him—for example, H. A. Simon, *Administrative Behavior* (New York: Macmillan, 1947), and P. Selznick, *T.V.A. and the Grass Roots* (Berkeley and Los Angeles: University of California Press, 1949), have in turn influenced me. The second invaluable book is the brilliant volume by Thomas C. Schelling, *The Strategy of Conflict*

(Cambridge, Mass.: Harvard University Press, 1960). Three other books which are especially good in conveying an understanding of organization are: Richard Neustadt, *Presidential Power* (New York: John Wiley & Sons, 1960); Herbert Kaufman's study of the forest service, *The Forest Ranger* (Baltimore: Johns Hopkins University Press, 1960); and Victor A. Thompson's remarkable study of the OPA, *The Regulatory Process in OPA Rationing* (New York: King's Point Press, 1950).

Law. The contributions of Holmes and Pound to the development of Anglo-American jurisprudence are summed up in Julius Stone, *The Province and Function of Law* (Cambridge, Mass.: Harvard University Press, 1950).

Karl Llewellyn's *The Bramble Bush* (New York: Oceana Press, 1960) makes good reading. One of my favorite books on the nature of law is Edmond Cahn, *The Moral Decision* (Bloomington: Indiana University Press, 1955). On American lawyers, Alexis de Tocqueville, *Democracy in America,* Vol. I, Chap. 6, despite its age, justifies rereading. So does *Felix Frankfurter Reminisces* (New York: Reynal, 1960). On the more systematic side, two interesting essays by David Riesman are clearly superior: the first is, "Toward an Anthropological Science of Law and the Legal Profession," in *Individualism Reconsidered* (Glencoe, Ill.: Free Press, 1954), pp. 440-66; the more recent of the two, "Law and Sociology: Recruitment, Training and Colleagueship," in *Law and Sociology,* ed. W. M. Evan (Glencoe, Ill.: Free Press, 1962), mentions other current work on the legal profession. On judges, Jack Peltason, *Federal Courts in the Political Process* (Garden City: Doubleday, 1955), while brief, is excellent.

The impact of regulation upon attitudes is brought out well in Robert E. Lane's "Law and Opinion in the Business Community," *Public Opinion Quarterly,* 17 (1953), 239-57, and "Why Business Men Violate the Law," *Journal of Criminal Law, Criminology and Police Science,* 44 (1953), 151-65, as well as in his *The Regulation of Businessmen* (New Haven: Yale University Press, 1954). Robert A. Dahl, *Who Governs?* (New Haven: Yale University Press, 1961), has a stimulating last chapter in which he speculates about the role of judges in the political process. Then of course there are Gordon Patric's description of "The Impact of a Court Decision: Aftermath of the McCollum Case," *Journal of Public Law,* 6 (1957), 455-63, and Frank Sorauf's "Zorach v. Clauson: The Impact of a Supreme Court Decision," *American Political Science Review,* 53 (1959), 777-91. Finally, one should read Benjamin Nathan Cardozo, *The Nature of the Judicial Process* (New Haven: Yale University Press, 1921), which for all its antiquity has no equal in literary grace and which contains a few very stimulating passages about the law's effect.

Supreme Court. One should start, it seems to me, with Charles Evans Hughes, *The Supreme Court of the United States* (Garden City: Garden City, 1936). A. M. Bickel, *The Least Dangerous Branch* (Indianapolis: Bobbs-Merrill, 1962), is eminently worthwhile, but Paul Freund's collection of essays, *The Supreme Court of the United States* (Cleveland: Meridian Books, 1961), is my favorite reading on the Court. C. H. Pritchett, *Congress versus the Supreme Court* (Minneapolis: University of Minnesota Press, 1961), is not Pritchett's best book, but is interesting in describing some of the tensions which exist between the judiciary and the legislature. The work of G. Schubert [e.g., *Constitutional Politics* (New York: Holt, Rinehart & Winston, 1960)] is the best embodiment of the effort to conceptualize and operationalize the factors which bring about Supreme Court decisions. The most illuminating literature of all on the Supreme Court is the opinions themselves. In the area of church and state, Joseph Tussman has edited a collection of opinions which he entitled *The Supreme Court on Church and State* (New York: Oxford University Press, 1962). For legal analysis of the *Schempp* opinion, one would do well to start with L. H. Pollak, "Foreword: Public Prayers in Public Schools," *Harvard Law Review,* 77 (1963), 62 ff.

Schools. N. Gross, W. S. Mason, and A. M. McEachern, *Explorations in Role Analysis: Studies of the School Superintendency Role* (New York: John Wiley & Sons, 1958), provides a superb glimpse of the school superintendent's function in a school system. Interesting and useful on school systems generally is P. R. Mort and F. G. Cornell, *American Schools in Transition* (New York: Teachers College, Columbia University, 1941). On the relations between the school system and the community during a debate involving religion and the schools, one might take a look at T. Powell, *The School Bus Law* (Middletown, Conn.: Wesleyan University Press, 1960).

Update. Several interesting books have been published since 1965 on the social impact of law. Two depict contrasting reactions to *Schempp*: Kenneth M. Dolbeare and Phillip E. Hammond, *The School Prayer Decisions* (Chicago: University of Chicago Press, 1971) and Richard M. Johnson, *The Dynamics of Compliance* (Evanston, Ill.: Northwestern University Press, 1967). Two engrossing books on the effect of civil rights legislation in the South are Frederick M. Wirt, *Politics of Southern Equality: Law and Social Change in a Mississippi County* (Chicago: Aldine, 1970) and Harrell R. Rodgers, Jr., and Charles S. Bullock III, *Law and Social Change: Civil Rights Laws and Their Consequences* (New York: McGraw-Hill, 1972).

Index